The Four Little Girls
and
Desire Caught by the Tail

T0352631

The Four Little Girls

and

Desire Caught by the Tail

Pablo Picasso

Translated by Roland Penrose

ALMA CLASSICS

ALMA CLASSICS
an imprint of

ALMA BOOKS LTD
Thornton House
Thornton Road
Wimbledon Village
London SW19 4NG
United Kingdom
www.almaclassics.com
www.101pages.co.uk

The Four Little Girls and *Desire Caught by the Tail* first published in
French by Editions Gallimard in 1949 and 1945 respectively, as
Les Quatre Petites Filles and *Le Désir attrapé par la queue*. These
translations first published separately by Calder & Boyars Ltd in 1970.
This edition first published by Alma Books Ltd in 2019
Reprinted 2024

Le Désir attrapé par la queue © Editions Gallimard, Paris, 1945 renou-
velé en 1972
Les Quatre Petites Filles © Editions Gallimard, Paris, 1968

Introduction and Translation © The estate of Roland Penrose, 1970,
2019

FSC
www.fsc.org

MIX
Paper | Supporting
responsible forestry
FSC® C013604

Printed in Great Britain by CPI Group (UK) Ltd, Croydon CR0 4YY

ISBN: 978-1-84749-802-1

Contents

Introduction

THE FOUR LITTLE GIRLS

Anyone who wishes to form an idea of the main themes that have occupied the imagination of Picasso throughout his long and astonishingly productive life will realize that, over and above the many problems of aesthetics, the invention of new styles such as cubism, the intense pleasures of new and startling combinations of colour, the abstract enjoyment of geometric and organic form and the revelations, illusions and metamorphoses achieved in objects and sculptures that bring into question the nature of reality itself, none of these delights germane to the visual arts can diminish Picasso's passionate involvement with the human presence, not only in its appearance, but more profoundly in its very nature and its daily behaviour. This being so, it is not surprising to find a ceaseless, eager inquiry into that most mysterious and intriguing period of life, childhood. But we learn from early drawings of urchins in the streets of Barcelona and the numerous mother-and-child paintings of the Blue Period that the child to whom Picasso was most attracted was not a sanctified bambino nor a Little Lord Fauntleroy, but rather the unselfconscious product of human life, the child of the people, innocent and yet stuffed to bursting with the germs of all the vices and virtues of an adult.

There are, however, among his early works in particular many drawings that show Picasso's desire to understand with accuracy the inquisitive gaze of the street urchin, and also there are paintings that convince us equally of the pleasure he found in the frolics and the fantasies in which little girls delight.

There is a small painting dating from about 1900 of three little red-haired nymphs in lace frocks and button boots dancing wildly together in a green field that recalls at once our *Alice in Wonderland*. Also, there is a more sober portrait of 1901, now in the Fogg Art Museum at Harvard, of another Alice-like girl demurely showing off her finery in a pink dress, wearing a large and very decorative hat.

This interest in the children of his friends and others seen more casually in the streets recurs periodically in Picasso's work, but happens most abundantly at moments when he was able to watch his own children at home, invent toys for them and enter into their most inconsequential games. Even before Picasso had any children of his own, there are paintings of the Circus Period in which Harlequin, a character with whom Picasso in his youth found close affinity, is surrounded by his family. The circus troupe is often accompanied by children and circus animals who are learning to find their liberation in the dangerous antics of the acrobat. Later, in the early Twenties, his own son Paul appears dressed ready for a masked ball in the gay costumes of Pierrot, Harlequin or a young torero. These are followed ten years later by drawings and paintings of his daughter Maia dressed in bright cotton frocks with a rag doll, sometimes adorning her hair, dancing, singing or asleep.

But the period of the most exuberant interest in children began after the last war. It came as a contrast to the years which began with the brutalities of the Spanish Civil War, to which Picasso reacted in his mural *Guernica*. In this great work he calls attention with eloquence to the proximity of the child to death in those catastrophic times, and in the many studies he made for it he shows the mother holding her dead babe in her arms as a reproach and a reminder of the intermingling throughout of love, death and life, a theme we find again in *The Four Little Girls*.

It was in 1946 that Picasso was once more able to return to his native Mediterranean after the tension of years of anxiety and privation spent in occupied Paris. A new atmosphere of Arcadian delight penetrated his work on the Provençal coast, where he went to live with Françoise Gilot, the mother of their two children, Claude and Paloma. In these surroundings Picasso brought back into his work the mythical population of fauns, centaurs, winged horses, doves, owls, goats and all the descendants of classical tradition, creating a world of fantasy or super-reality which we recognize as an inseparable part of our lives when we live fully. The world of his imagination was again tinged with rosy-fingered dawn, but also linked to the familiar realities of daily life seen with precise and penetrating observation.

The protean qualities and talents of Picasso are proverbial, and his work provides innumerable examples of his ability to turn without hesitation from one mode of expression to another. Since during his life he has had more intimate friendships with poets than with painters, it was natural that he should one day turn to writing poetry himself. This happened in the autumn of 1935, when an emotional crisis had discouraged him from painting. Long and extraordinary poems were published in the *Cahiers d'Art* (Nos. 7–10, 1935), with enthusiastic articles by André Breton and other surrealists, who realized that Picasso's contribution to literature was more than a passing experiment. In his language there was the same richness of imagery and daring as there was in his use of visual media. His disregard for punctuation and syntax was as complete as had been his revolutionary attitude towards academic conventions in painting. It resulted in a new language, conveying a new and vivid vision of reality.

At a time when the misery of war lay heavily on the French, Picasso produced unexpectedly a short play in six acts, *Desire Caught by the Tail*, which greatly delighted his friends. Writing rapidly, he condensed in it the sordid realities of the time with irony, wit and a flood of extraordinary images. Its atmosphere is in sharp contrast with the radiant absurdities of the four little girls who became the actors of the play Picasso wrote at a more idyllic time four years later.

The world of Picasso, whether it be the gloom of occupied Paris or the Arcadian sunshine of the Mediterranean, is populated by both gods and devils. The cold, the darkness and the anxiety of the first play have melted into the fresh perfumed air of a Provençal kitchen garden, but the little girls have not become angels, nor is their innocence untroubled. Their violent yearnings and desires are expressed in a brilliant flow of images, disconnected in their childish exuberance. The first little girl sets the pace, saying, "Let us play at hurting ourselves and hug each other with fury making horrible noises", adding later, with surprising insight, "make the best you can of life. As for me, I wrap the chalk of my desires in a cloak, torn and covered with black-ink stains that drip full-throated from blind hands searching for the mouth of the wound."

In contrast to this poetic melancholy, there are scenes of wild childish enjoyment, singing and dancing, in which the fourth little girl declares "in all our caperings we are going to shout aloud the joy of being alone and mad". In a language which is both innocent and sophisticated, using words and idioms that have a genuine ring of childish nonsense, the girls expound at length their fantasies, their dreams of shipwrecks, their conversations with flowers, birds and animals, their mockery of adults, their visions of all-pervading colour, delicious combinations of coloured sweetmeats, wine and the merry-go-round at the fair. With innocent wisdom they speak in turn like a Greek chorus:

SECOND LITTLE GIRL: Only the eye of the bull that dies
in the arena sees.
FIRST LITTLE GIRL: It sees itself.
FOURTH LITTLE GIRL: The deforming mirror sees.
SECOND LITTLE GIRL: Death, that clear water...
FIRST LITTLE GIRL: And very heavy.

Beneath the buffoonery and spontaneous joy of these four
charming and precocious children runs the current of their
main preoccupation with instinctive desires and fears: love,
death and life.

As in *Desire Caught by the Tail*, the stage directions are
of great importance, but difficult to carry out literally in a
conventional theatre. Picasso seems to have had in mind a
play which could be more easily read than acted – but it is
in these directions that we see most clearly the extent of his
memory. For instance, in the fourth act we find: "Enter an
enormous winged white horse dragging its guts, surrounded
by eagles: an owl is perched on its head..." This is not only
an allusion to the bullfight, as we will see later, but also to
the winged white horse that appeared on the drop-curtain
of the Diaghilev ballet *Parade*, painted by Picasso in 1915.
In the same curtain there is a tall ladder on which a little
winged girl is climbing. The owl is also one of Picasso's
oldest and most persistent images.

There are however many allusions and puns which have a
more immediate origin in the jokes and distortions of words
that Picasso picked up from listening to and playing with
his own children. These inventions were often the result of a
game of words played between them while he was writing the
play. On this occasion he spent more time than he had done
on *Desire Caught by the Tail*, and often read passages to his
children and even to visitors. It can be seen throughout how
close and persistent was his observation of children. It was
important for him to understand their imaginary world and

their habits in this case, just as it had been all his life. There is no more convincing example of the importance he attached to this, and of his own humility before the wonder of their vision, than the remark he made to Herbert Read when they met at an exhibition of children's drawings. "When I was their age," he said, "I could draw like Raphael, but it took me a lifetime to learn to draw like them." (Herbert Read, Letter to *The Times*, 26th October 1956.)

As often happens with Picasso, the current of his thought continued after writing this play in drawings of little girls dancing a round. These were followed by studies for the murals *War* and *Peace*, painted for the deconsecrated chapel in Vallauris, which were not finished until 1951. In the panel dedicated to *Peace*, we find again the winged horse, now diligently ploughing the soil, and allusions to the little girls in figures dancing to the music of a flute, while in the panel *War* are the monsters that threaten all innocence and tranquillity. There is the same basic contrast between the two panels, the same dichotomy and unity of no good without evil, no evil without good that occurs throughout beneath the charm and cruelty of the play, which is summarized in the stage directions at the end, where the girls "lie down on the ground and go to sleep. Some trees, flowers, fruits; everywhere blood is flowing: it makes pools and inundates the stage."

A disconcerting factor which must finally be mentioned is the anonymity throughout of the four participants. The third little girl exists only by her elusive cries offstage until near the end of the play, when she suddenly emerges naked from the well. All four are symbols of the child. Their individual characteristics appear only intermittently, and it is from this that an atmosphere of timelessness emerges, and the wonder and horror of childhood is shown to us in all its tangle of brilliant intuition and spontaneity. The child, like Picasso himself, is exploring the illusions and realities of a new world.

DESIRE CAUGHT BY THE TAIL

Is it because life is too short and human powers too limited that poets are not often painters or painters poets, or is there some contradiction between qualities needed in artist and poet which presents visual sensibility and powers of verbal expression from existing in the same man? In general it seems that those who – like the painter – live most acutely by the aid of their eyes tend to be unable to express themselves in words, while those who can write down their thoughts are often incapable of using the plastic arts as a medium, so that it might be supposed that a damming-up of the means of expression in the one case will lead to an overflowing exuberance and clarity in the other. In any case, disapproval is usually expressed by the critics when an artist dabbles in a sphere which is not considered to be his own – and, indeed, few have found the time and the energy to make more than an occasional sally into the territories of another art.

We can think of the drawings of Victor Hugo and Lewis Carroll, the sonnets of Michelangelo, but it was particularly Leonardo who transgressed in this way, and his answer to "foolish folk" who criticized him is of particular interest: "I am fully aware that the fact of my not being a man of letters may cause certain arrogant persons to think that they may with reason censure me… They will say that because of my lack of book learning, I cannot properly express what I desire to treat of. Do they not know that my subjects require for their exposition experience rather than the words of others? And since experience has been the mistress of whoever has written well, I take her as my mistress, and to her in all points make my appeal."

This attitude rules out the dilettante approach of those who take up some art as a part-time hobby – professional men, statesmen, doctors and others who adopt an art as a kind of occupational therapy. This is not enough. To the artist all branches of the arts carry with them the same poetic reality, and it is only because of an overwhelming desire for total expression that one art can be called upon to fulfil the deficiencies of another. In a preface to Picasso's poems in the *Cahiers d'Art* in 1935, Breton pointed out that Picasso has always expressed himself poetically, and the deliberate choice of using words rather than another medium has the same heroic quality that is found in the great strength and originality of vision of his plastic works. In fifty years of the most powerful creative production that we know of in our time, Picasso has been the leader of a revolution in the arts. "An enterprise such as this requires all the resources of a passion which is self-sufficient, which disposes of a thousand tongues of fire."

There is no barrier between the arts for Picasso. With prodigious talent, he has explored the possibilities of sculpture, photography, ceramics, lithography, and has in each case brought his own inventions and understood how to use the unfamiliar art so as to express more vigorously the drama of his perception of everyday life. Musicians are among his closest friends, and his love of music is expressed in the frequent appearance of musical instruments, particularly guitars and flutes, in his paintings. The period when his association with musicians was closest was that brilliant epoch of the Russian Ballet, when, under the direction of Sergei Diaghilev, ballets such as *Parade* and *Pulcinella*, with Picasso's scenery and costumes, reached a rare perfection and showed the profound emotional effect that can be attained by a close collaboration between the arts.

Picasso has always been on intimate terms with a large circle of poets and authors. His friend and biographer Jaime Sabartés describes how, in a conversation at Royan in the early days of the Second World War, he said:

"When reading, you often notice that the author would have wished to paint and not write. One divines from the pleasure he takes in describing, as though painting, what he says – a landscape or a character – that he really would prefer to be using a paintbrush and colours... Maillol, for instance, did not realize, to begin with, his vocation as a sculptor, as happens to many others. Some painters find their path from sculpture, and many politicians would have sacrificed half their celebrity and their lives to devote the other half to literature." Sabartés goes on to say that the next day, when he paid Picasso a visit, he found that the usual daily output of new drawings and paintings had been stopped for a bout of writing.

Just as when a sculptor turns to painting we can trace in his works the sculptor's preoccupation with form, so the painter's poem will contain unusually vivid plastic imagery. "He is a dream repainted in watercolour on a pearl. His hair has the intricate arabesques of the halls in the palace of the Alhambra." Picasso's poetry contains a torrent of metaphor, and the most unorthodox juxtaposition of words piled together creates in the mind visions of wide and varied appeal. There is an appeal to all the senses. In the following passage, taken from *Desire Caught by the Tail*, it is sound that dominates the atmosphere. "The noise of unfastened shutters, hitting their drunken bells on the crumpled sheets of the stones, tears from the night despairing cries of pleasure." French shutters banging their hearts out against stone walls during the darkness of a winter storm, crumpled sheets, tears and cries of pleasure... the picture grows – it is a living picture: the stones beaten by the shutters are associated with the crumpled sheets. It is as though these objects and passions infect each other and live in each other's attributes.

The same metamorphosis takes place frequently in modern painting. It can be seen clearly in Picasso's above-mentioned mural *Guernica,* where the eyes of the women are shaped like tears, their pointed tongues are like knives piercing the air, the flames from the houses are like the crests of cocks and the dying horse has the surface of a bare field of stubble, while its mouth is like a fortress firing its last defiant salvo. This world of association is inherent in the forms, which echo meanings beyond those they are obviously intended to represent.

Throughout *Desire Caught by the Tail*, language is forced into the same service. The dreamlike sense which flows from Big Foot's soliloquies comes from the influence of one word upon its unlikely neighbours. Language has been forced into a state of instability, and like a spring uncoils with violence, hitting out on all sides as it is released. What style could be more suitable to Picasso in expressing the rage, the anxiety and the nostalgia he felt during the Nazi occupation of Paris in the depths of the blackest winter of the war?

The play is a burlesque and often riotously funny, but as Jean Cassou remarks, "Death is always present in the solitudes and caprices of the Spaniards." The wildest scenes of enjoyment end again and again in disaster. After the opening discussion between the characters, who are well feasted and ready to explain the primary truths to their cousin, the Curtains shake themselves with a night of thunder in their incongruous belly, and the stage is flooded with will-o'-the-wisps. In Act Two their picnic ends with the arrival of undertakers, who bring in coffins, into which they pack everybody, nail them down and carry them off. Act Three finishes with Big Foot's admirers covered with blood and fainting on the floor. After universal and unprecedented success in the lottery – in which all the characters, including the Curtains themselves, become millionaires – Act Four ends with the fumes of chipped potatoes filling the room, until complete suffocation follows. Finally, the prize-giving and dancing in the last act is interrupted by a golden ball the size of a man bursting in at the window and blinding the entire cast.

The way in which annihilation recurs – and still the play continues – has its parallel in the successive deaths of the bull in a bullfight, when each time the spectators rise to their feet in reverence and then settle down again to see the same drama re-enacted. There is no unravelling of a plot. The sequence of the scenes and the coming and going of the characters suggest more the form of a ballet than a drama. The scenes in the corridor of Sordid's Hotel and the closing act are frankly like a ballet in conception. Another allusion to the bullfight comes in Big Foot's reflection: "The guts which Pegasus drags behind him after the fight draw her portrait on the whiteness and hardness of the gleaming marble of her sorrow." This is clearly the imagery of a painter, a sculptor and a Spaniard.

Picasso has usually written in Spanish. This play, designed for the amusement of his French friends, whose lot he was sharing, was written in French, but the language, as well as the images and background, have a strong savour of his native land. Here is another example which shows clearly the plastic qualities of the painter's vision: "The titillations of crows that make the jagged wheel of the machine for sewing and unsewing buttons animate the half-dead landscape so little that grass grows over their flight and at the shadows carried by their wings fail to stick on the wall of the church, but slip along the cobble stones of the square, where they break to pieces."

Throughout *Desire Caught by the Tail* there is an animism which not only makes living characters of the Curtains, the feet with their screaming chilblains, the Onion, the Tart, Silence and Anxiety, but also brings to life domestic objects and even their clothes. Thin Anxiety finds her white-lace ball dress "writhing in burning pain under the dust".

But in spite of the richness of the imagery and the wideness of its poetic echoes, there is no romantic tenderness. The pitch of irony, the wildness of the caprices, springing as they do from the experiences of the appalling realities of the time, reach a point where our only possible reaction is a burst of bitter laughter. The experiences are not only of war, love and Sordid's Hotel, but of everyday people and objects all living together as companions and characters in the same drama. It is a play of misery, discomfort, anguish, hunger and passion caught in the impossibility of its fulfilment.

The Tart gives us a clue when she says, "You know, I have found love. He has all the skin worn off his knees and goes begging from door to door. He hasn't got a farthing, and is looking for a job as a suburban bus conductor. It is sad, but go to his help... he'll turn on you and sting you." But the situations that arise are full of a riotous humour and are a mockery of the daily trials of the time. The dominating theme naturally is food. Big Foot, in praise of his girlfriend the Tart, woos her, saying, "your buttocks [are] a plate of cassoulet, and your arms a soup of sharks' fins, and your... and your nest of swallows still the fire of swallow's nest soup", and he declares that "nothing is as good as mutton stew ... on a wonderful day when it is snowing hard". When the Anxiety sisters sit down to their stew of Spanish melon, palm oil, broad beans, salt, vinegar and breadcrumbs, "the great bouquet of terror and frights already begins to wave us goodbye". Thin Anxiety finds that she is "nothing but a congealed soul, stuck to the window panes of the fire" and that "the old sewing machine which turns the horses and the lions of the tangled merry-go-round of my desires chops up my sausage flesh and offers it alive to the ice-cold hands of stillborn stars, tapping on the panes of my window their wolfish hunger and their oceanic thirst". Fat Anxiety appears all dishevelled and black with dirt, rising from the bedlinen full of potato chips, holding an old frying pan, but the manner of address is on a very different plane:

THIN ANXIETY: The sun.
FAT ANXIETY: Love.
THIN ANXIETY: Aren't you beautiful!

Our passionate hero Big Foot, as well as having a great appetite, is also no mean author, as we see when he produces a fine surprise for the Tart – his novel – and serves her with a slice of the "great sausage" taken from page 380,000. He seeks throughout to embellish his lecherous passion, lighting "the candles of sin with the match of her charms", in extravagant metaphors and paradox, and finally proclaims through music as the play draws to a close: "Let us wrap the worn-out sheets in the face-powder of angels... Throw flights of doves with all our strength against the bullets and lock securely the houses demolished by bombs" – a mock-heroic Chaplinesque effort to put things right by doing the wrong thing.

The play is characteristically dated in the same way that Picasso dates his canvases and drawings even when he does not trouble to sign them, giving them the significance of a daily commentary on the events that have contributed to their creation.

It took him from Tuesday 14th January to Friday 17th January 1941 to sketch out this violent picture of the life around him. But it was not until 19th March 1944 that Picasso's friends were able to give a first reading under the noses of the Nazis, who would have taken action against all concerned if they had discovered what was in progress. Here is the notice that appeared later in the journal *Messages,* Cahier II, 1944:

"On 19th March 1944, at the house of Michel Leiris, a public reading was given of *Desire Caught by the Tail*, directed and produced by Albert Camus. The cast was as follows: Mmes Zanie Aubier (the Tart), Simone de Beauvoir (her Cousin), Dora Maar (Thin Anxiety), Germaine Hugnet (Fat Anxiety), Louise Leiris (the Two Bow-Wows), MM. Michel Leiris (Big Foot), Jean-Paul Sartre (Round Piece), Raymond Queneau (the Onion), Jacques Bost (Silence), Jean Aubier (the Curtains). George Hugnet in charge of the musical accompaniment."

The readers, seated in an arc like a Cuadro Flamenco, with Camus standing in a corner reading the stage directions, rose in turn to speak their words, while the music came from a gramophone in a neighbouring room. About 120 people attended, and among the audience were many distinguished artists, musicians, writers and actors, including Jean-Louis Barrault, Armand Salacrou, Paul Éluard and Picasso himself. The success of this first reading was so great that it was repeated five or six times, and according to Michel Leiris it gave those present a feeling of an affirmation of liberty.

The same type of reading, from a translation, was given in London three years later at the London Gallery in Brook Street, and again it proved extremely successful. Although it might be possible to stage the play in a more conventional way, the best effect can be achieved by a reading without scenery or costumes. This formula, admirable in its economy, calls upon the imagination of the audience in the same way as did Elizabethan drama with its sign boards instead of scenery.

A second reading was given in London in February 1950 at the Rudolf Steiner Hall, organized by the Institute of Contemporary Arts. The leading parts were taken by Valentine Dyall as Big Foot and Dylan Thomas as the Onion.

This was followed by a reading of William Blake's *An Island in the Moon* – a work that bears interesting similarities to Picasso's play in terms of form and humour – in which Dylan Thomas took the leading role.

One of the most valuable aspects of this short play is that it helps us to see from a new angle the intimate processes of Picasso's creation. The verbal picture is as generous and original in its associations as the colour and form of his paintings. Realism is attained by looking "behind the behind of the story which so deeply interests and grieves us" and by the animation of objects combined with the process in which thoughts and abstract ideas take shape or become live personalities. "The galloping pace of his love, the canvas born each morning in the fresh egg of his nakedness, crystallized into thought, jumps the barrier and falls panting on the bed. I have such marks on my body; they are alive; they shout and sing and prevent me from catching the eight forty-five." There is no abstraction in Picasso's mind, and this is true of all his work, both plastic and literary – there is no idea of withdrawing into a quiet contemplation of static, frozen beauty. On the contrary, he humanizes and gives life to the world within, as well as the objects of the world without, and in this audacious process of calling together a picture with wide sweeps of his wand Picasso the magician pauses to smile or wink at his audience.

– Roland Penrose

The Four Little Girls
and
Desire Caught by the Tail

THE FOUR LITTLE GIRLS

Characters

ACT ONE

ACT ONE

Scene: A kitchen garden – a well almost in the centre.

FOUR LITTLE GIRLS (*singing*):
>We won't go to the woods
>The laurels all are cut
>That honey there
>Will go and pick them up
>Let's go to the dance
>This is how they dance.
>Dancing, singing, kissing whoever you will.

FIRST LITTLE GIRL: Let us open all the roses with our nails and make their perfumes bleed on the wrinkles of fire, of games, of our songs and of our yellow, blue and purple aprons. Let's play at hurting ourselves and hug each other with fury making horrible noises.

SECOND LITTLE GIRL: Mummy, Mummy, come and see Yvette ransacking the garden and setting the butterflies on fire, Mummy, Mummy!

THIRD LITTLE GIRL: Decide for yourselves how you want to light the cock's feather flames of the candles among the diapers hung on the branches of the cherry trees. Be careful, I am telling you, of the wings detached from dead caged birds, singing in full flight on the shot silk sleeves of a dress pleated with sky that has fallen out of the blue.

FIRST LITTLE GIRL (*singing*):
>We won't go to the woods
>The laurels all are cut
>That honey there…

5

(*She shouts.*)

> There, there, there, the cat has taken one of the birds
> from the nest in its jaws and strangles it with its big
> fingers carrying it off behind a lemon-coloured cloud,
> stolen from the melted butter of the part of the wall
> that the ashen sun has knocked flat.

THIRD LITTLE GIRL: Isn't she stupid?

FOURTH LITTLE GIRL: Decide for yourselves all of you
about the flowers. The knitting-wool is dragging its
feet all over the garden and hangs its rosary of quick
glances on each branch and glasses full of wine in the
crystal of organs that can be heard tapping close at
hand on the cotton wool of the sky hidden behind great
rhubarb leaves.

FIRST LITTLE GIRL: Make the best you can, make the best
you can of life. As for me, I wrap the chalk of my desires
in a cloak, torn and covered with black-ink stains that
drip full-throated from blind hands searching for the
mouth of the wound.

THIRD LITTLE GIRL (*hidden behind the well*): Coming,
coming, coming.

FIRST, SECOND AND FOURTH LITTLE GIRLS: Stupid,
stupid, you are stupid, you are doubly visible, you can be
seen all naked covered with a rainbow. Tidy your hair, it
is in flames and is going to set fire to the chain of curtsies
scratched in the tousled wig of bells licked by the mistral.

THIRD LITTLE GIRL: Coming, coming, coming. You won't
get me alive and you can't see me. I am dead.

FOURTH LITTLE GIRL: Don't be an idiot!

FIRST LITTLE GIRL: If you don't come back, we shall all
go and hang ourselves from the lemon trees and live our
dramas in flowers and our dances on the knife-edge of
our tears.

SECOND LITTLE GIRL: We are going to bring you a ladder.

(*They fetch a long ladder and carry it, held upright with difficulty.*)

FIRST LITTLE GIRL: No, she is behind the well. No, she is on the roof of the house.

FOURTH LITTLE GIRL: She is on the branch with the flowers up there to the left of the pear tree.

SECOND LITTLE GIRL: I see her hand biting the end of the wing of a leaf that bleeds.

FOURTH LITTLE GIRL: No, no, she is in front of the reddish-brown stain that makes a bugle call on the window of the room upstairs, scalding with punches a broken corner of the blinded sun trying to find his way in darkness.

FIRST LITTLE GIRL: She crawls along, she seems to be looking between the damp leaves and the herbs for her lunch, unrolling her arabesques in curves and colours and gossamer threads.

FOURTH LITTLE GIRL: Will you please come along, Paulette, yes or no? You are a pain in the neck. I would like to tell Mummy that you don't want to play and that you want to show off by changing, in a thousand different ways, into a bouquet of japanese flowers.

SECOND LITTLE GIRL: Let them do what they like! I gather grapefruit, I eat them, I spit out the pips, I wipe my lips with the back of my hand and I light up the festoons of lanterns with my laugh, incomparable cheeses, I ask you to accept yours sincerely at your feet and I sign.

FIRST LITTLE GIRL: It is really difficult to spend a pleasant summer afternoon with you and it's more and more and more obvious that you won't play at anything which touches chronologically on the lessons that we have been given at ears' length in class all winter.

SECOND LITTLE GIRL: We must leave her and not worry about her, she will come back, her craftiness all subdued, and make us laugh with her sham account books and her ingenious arrangements, however artistic they be.

(FIRST, SECOND AND FOURTH LITTLE GIRLS. *A long silence – three minutes; holding the ladder with much difficulty, they go round in silence from one corner of the stage to another, bringing it near to the trees, to the walls of the house, and trying to get it near and to put it into the well; during this time the voice of the* THIRD LITTLE GIRL *is heard.*)

THIRD LITTLE GIRL: Coming, coming, coming, coming.

(*It begins to rain.*)

SECOND LITTLE GIRL: It's raining, it's soggy
    It's the fate of old froggy
    It's raining, it's soggy...
FOURTH LITTLE GIRL: It's raining, it's soggy
    It's the fate of old froggy...
THIRD LITTLE GIRL: Coming...
SECOND LITTLE GIRL: You mustn't believe that the cat has gone off behind the carrots to eat its eagle without fear or remorse. The blue of its cry for pity, the mauve of its leaps and the violent violets of its claws tearing Veronese-green rays from the sulphur-yellow of its rage, detached from the blood spurting from the fountain full of vermilion, the ochre of the lilac wall and the sharp cobalt fringes of its cries, the poor bird crouching on the clogs of its feathers, acrobatic monkey, the flags smacking their tongues on the steel and the knife already embedded, the cat gathers together and lets go its shadows and its swords on each floor, confused and

confounded in the fall of verticals squashing themselves drop by drop on the olive-green curtain.

FIRST LITTLE GIRL: It's raining, it's soggy,
It's the fate of old froggy.
It's raining, it's soggy,
It's the fate of old froggy.
It's raining, it snows,
It's the fate of the bedbug.

SECOND LITTLE GIRL: I wish she would come back. We miss the sun, it's raining. The laughter of the flowers is tearing the dress with the white and verdigris checks and bursting the heart of the cloth crucified on my sandals with acrobatics and crabby temper. Call her, Jeannette, give a great shout, so that she takes her place in the sun again and pull the plumb line through the wrong end of the opera glasses.

FIRST LITTLE GIRL: Let her alone and say nothing. Silence should lay its egg on the square of her fate broken to pieces by the game of the great curves thrown at great expense over the windmills with numerous intrigues their wings clipped of all laurels and very happy to be out of trouble at such small cost.

SECOND LITTLE GIRL: You won't make me believe – and if I say believe I exaggerate – that her departure and the synthetic projection of her image, even diluted in the imaginary broth of this afternoon, is subject to the following dazzling revelations and audacious cursory discussions.

FIRST LITTLE GIRL: The rain which rises little by little lasts ten centuries already and composes meticulously the page painted so minutely with little signs and squiggles coming undone and Gordian knots and anthropometric pegs, all responsibilities and consequences of the game imposed by the other side of the river – that's where she has given us so much pleasure...

FOURTH LITTLE GIRL: She has sunk us and doesn't realize that for us it's raining, that it's freezing, that the sun is lying flat on the ground, that we walk on it, that we burn ourselves.

SECOND LITTLE GIRL: The birds have horns, the flowers are chewing their fingernails and the clouds are being used to clean the window panes. It is stiflingly hot in paradise, and the birds are already setting the clouds on fire.

FIRST LITTLE GIRL: The flowers smell the soup that my aunt has on the stove for dinner since five o'clock yesterday evening and which at ten minutes to seven the wide-open door of our weeping carried with staring eyes all souls aboard the paroxysm yes – no – yes – I don't know. But the fine weather again takes over and tickles its palette filled to the brim from a load of stained glass drunk to the dregs.

FOURTH LITTLE GIRL: It's stopped raining, we can play. Let's run round the well, let's have fun, let's play the fool. The branch of the pear tree has smacked that great pile of clouds, and the toe of the palm tree's shoe snores crouched on the tablecloth, mouse grubbing out its lice. Let's run like mad things, like lunatics, and carry off with us all the flowers, the blondes and the brunettes, the sweet and the bitter, the tender and the hard in stone and in cotton wool, in oil and vinegar, in Chinese ink and invisible ink, without a spelling mistake and with forty-five thousand commas. Let's go and run, play, go mad…

(*Dancing*)

…mad – mad – mad – mad – mad – mad – mad – mad…

FIRST LITTLE GIRL: Black the leaves of the kitchen garden are going to write their life in a flash, the branches will dream of the arches of the future and will be gentle and well behaved like votive images and, although they look noisy and although their breath is homely, comfortably seated in front of the fire reading the paper they will mark up the acts of fate on a slate. Attack of memories with folded arms unwinds its music in acid, the great winged sheep far away rings its bell.

SECOND LITTLE GIRL: Isn't it lovely here, and isn't it lovely in the country, in the sun, your big tummy all melting in the middle, playing, playing and giggling in the sun stuffed with mulberries, the sun full of ribbons, full of pebbles, full of ice-cream cones. Let's all go and laugh and sing and have din-dins.

FOURTH LITTLE GIRL: Bring your pieces of coloured glass and find the cuttlefish bone which do as a plate. The russet feathers of the dry branches, olive stones and shells from my necklace with cinders from the great wall of plane trees will oil the slice of brown bread from the fruit bowl caught in a trap by the fountain. Go and find the black silk veil with which we can cover ourselves all over so as to act the wedding night that we are going to spend at the bottom of the well full of fried stars. Jeannette's mummy, the evening of my sister's wedding, had on a dress embroidered with coloured electric-light bulbs. Go and see if the trees are already in bed and asleep. We must make as much noise as possible, and in all our caperings we are going to shout aloud the joy of being alone and mad. We are going to hang the ladder on the tree, and we are going to light our kitchen fire on each leaf, which we will darn with cotton, branches, thorns of sugar, the bitter honey of the needles, the prickly double eucalyptus flowers.

(*They take a ladder and hook it to the top branches of the tree, lying on their stomachs on the ground, and going to sleep the voice is heard of the...*)

THIRD LITTLE GIRL: Coming, coming, coming...

FIRST, SECOND AND FOURTH LITTLE GIRLS (*gets up and begins to dance round, jumping and singing*): Coming, coming, coming, coming. Let's go to war, war at home. Marshmallow angels, mice and rats, caramel night, jingle-bell morning. The bustle that goes on has made a mess in my sheets. Coming, coming, coming, coming. Life hides its vows to milk the cows. Life is fine, let's hide away from it. The calves are dead and have got wings. The wheel that turns undoes its dress and shows its breasts under the grass, the night hides its little fishes. The lovely turtle dove loves its turdle. Tell us, hollyhock, about this evening's sunrise, tell us a story and make us laugh, take off your ball and chain, untie your rosaries, play your pistol for us on this bouquet of miserere moss-roses, how happy we are, happy to be together tomorrow, the day after tomorrow, today and yesterday.

(*They turn round, jump and shout faster and faster, louder and louder, and laughing fall to the ground on top of each other.*)

FOURTH LITTLE GIRL: We had a good giggle. I giggle. You giggle. She giggles. Happy happy happy happy, I am happy.

SECOND LITTLE GIRL: Happy.

FIRST LITTLE GIRL: I am happy, I am happy.

(*They start shouting*:)

Coming, coming, coming.

(*And innumerable birds are heard singing, and a rain of eyes begins to fall on them, sticking to their hair and their dresses.*)

SECOND LITTLE GIRL: We are covered with light.

FOURTH LITTLE GIRL: We are dirty with light.

SECOND LITTLE GIRL: I am burnt.

FIRST LITTLE GIRL: I am frozen with light.

SECOND LITTLE GIRL: Look, look at the top of the ladder: a bird. It's tearing itself to bits, you can see its heart crying and its claws scratching out its eyes.

FOURTH LITTLE GIRL: The leaves around it are showing their wolf's teeth and threaten it with their gentle hands closed.

FIRST LITTLE GIRL: We must help it.

SECOND LITTLE GIRL: Don't touch it, it burns, it is on fire: a torch.

FIRST LITTLE GIRL: Let's tear all these eyes off our dresses or hide their stare under our hands.

FOURTH LITTLE GIRL: Let's wrap ourselves in the veil, let's frighten ourselves and make a hedge around us with a circle of knives stuck in the ground by their handles.

FIRST LITTLE GIRL: Let's throw the flowers in the garden at him so that he dies of laughter.

SECOND LITTLE GIRL: Let's act a play. Let's set the stage in front of the well and disguise the trees as waves. You, you'll be the shipwreck, you the thunder and lightning, and me the moon. You, you'll tell the waves to take off their nets and catch all the stars and the shells in their paws and throw them to us like pearl necklaces and march past on the blue table and the black chairs riding on cows and making faces. You, the smallest, you will offer them carrots, cabbages and tomatoes that we are going to gather on our knees singing, holding the veil by its four corners, and you, during all this, you will light a great bonfire and throw on it all our dresses. We shall be naked, and you too will undress at the same time, and we shall go and hide under the table. But take great care not to burn yourself in the fire. Don't get too near with your pitchers full of wine. Some big rhubarb leaves that we shall plait around it will make the blackest of curtains for the tender mercies that the storm will let loose on us when the waves come and seize us by the throat and wrap us up with their shrews. The greediest silence will fill its pitcher of fire, and the broken wings of the horse that drags its guts in the ashes will open their grenades to a mirror filled with moons. When at a sign you will show you are going to bite, we shall all get up, and we shall scratch our faces till they bleed. Then the honey from the well will disgorge all its bees, and, pretending to be dead with fright, we shall laugh and sing our heads off together. The ship which will come onto the stage with all sails set will be full of milk and blood and on fire, lit up by a thousand lanterns.

FOURTH LITTLE GIRL: Tell me, tell me, will the thunder and lightning laugh, laugh, be unhappy, will she be frightened, all naked in the sea under the table, will she be blonde and a redhead and tall with long black-and-amaranth-coloured hair, will she have a lover, don't tell me the truth but whopping lies, I want to see my hands, rummage in the thick mattress of stars thrown no matter how on the back of the sky, walking about on the edge of that crazy roof.

FIRST LITTLE GIRL: Finally, a mighty disappointment, spontaneously drawn up in intricate arabesques and mathematical circumvolutions. But the big question is to know if I am absolutely white, in swan's down, in pure white linen paper and entirely covered with snow and standing alone on the edge of the roof and immobile.

SECOND LITTLE GIRL: Shut up, you bore us!

FOURTH LITTLE GIRL: No, you will be the one who sees, and with your piece of chalk, with your eyes closed, you will draw the admiring glances of men everywhere.

FIRST LITTLE GIRL: Hide your hands behind your eyes and read the spring green future of leaves and flowers that water your hair with music.

SECOND LITTLE GIRL: I sing, I sing evening and morning, and I don't like fooling around, I only like the noisy refuge of the silence of my sinking ship, and catch! – it's the height of the season.

FOURTH LITTLE GIRL: Do you see...

FIRST LITTLE GIRL: Ha!

FOURTH LITTLE GIRL: Do re mi fa sol la ti do.

FIRST LITTLE GIRL: Do ti la sol fa me re do. There, a great sun slowly rolls across the stage to our feet, where it stretches out full length and licks our hands. Isn't he nice!

SECOND LITTLE GIRL: The distant flute takes to pieces the game of patience irrigating the colour and invents patiently the stage play with the great ship gliding amorously through the bridal veils of the wreck, scratching its fleas in the acid-drop blues of the azure, held in both hands on the pummel of the mare and catastrophically caught in a brief and fleeting run of luck.

FIRST LITTLE GIRL: The blue aims the point of its azureal bluish cloak, indigo, cobalt, sky-blue, plum, at the outstretched arms of lemon-yellow, almond-green and pistachio, encircling the lilac-mauve, hit with both fists by the green of the orange and the tablecloth with royal-blue and periwinkle-blue stripes, bursting in confusion at its knees, and all the acid-drop rainbow of the white boarded by the arch of wet feet in emerald-green, funambulesque sounds of a gong beaten to death among the skeins of carnations and such rambling roses.

FOURTH LITTLE GIRL: The blue, the blue, the azure, the blue, the blue of the white, the blue of the rose, lilac-blue, the blue of yellow, the blue of red, the blue of lemon, the blue orange, the blue that oozes from blue and the white blue, and the red blue and the blue of the palms from the lemon blue of white doves, to the jasmine in the fields of oats, in great almond, emerald-green songs.

SECOND LITTLE GIRL: Spirals of lemons, great white squares of oranges, lemon lozenges, perfect ovals, exasperated circles of lilac roses, of tomatoes sung, whispered by the olives of the violet hidden in mulberry syrup.

FIRST LITTLE GIRL: White, the red rose, the carnation, the blue, the white yellow flooding over the wall, spittle of the varnish of fire chained to steel bars, a long veil, dragged along by the immense wings of the little needle stuck into the cheek of the circle which bursts out in a dress spangled with brambles of lights.

SECOND LITTLE GIRL: Sweet afternoon, sweet, sweet, an afternoon of sweetness, sweet.

FOURTH LITTLE GIRL: Grandfather clock full of bees, isle of honey.

SECOND LITTLE GIRL: Ship full of bees suckling a flight of doves detached from their wings, carried away with great shouts of cars, games and capers of immaculate laughter and drunkenness.

FOURTH LITTLE GIRL: The twelve white winged horses that draw the coach made of a grain of rice inundate from their great blue, yellow and red jars the immensity of the plate full of golden sweets with a sheaf of acanthus leaves plaited round it, and jets of mercury from the fountain make their iridescent vapours and their melodies and naked swords of their songs.

SECOND LITTLE GIRL: Azure watermelon stuck all over the nails, scissors curring the woven threads of the river that drags its hair in the sand, its torn robe illegible to the ear of the broken charm, hobbling lamely on its long leg.

FIRST LITTLE GIRL: The great yellow oval struggles in silence between the two blue points of its claws, all bent double in a fall of Icarus into the skein of lines of air olive-green lozenge trap, strangled in both hands by the tender violet of the square of a vermilion arch thrown from so far away by the orange.

FOURTH LITTLE GIRL: Blue, pink, lilac, lemon-yellow, pistachio-green, the green of orange and the blue and violet, mauve and lilac and red.

SECOND LITTLE GIRL: My hand is full of voices, my hair is covered with ribbons of all colours. Comb them out. They slip between my fingers and light fireworks on each leaf torn from the tree by each thrust of the hips.

FIRST LITTLE GIRL: The golden dust which hangs on each sigh the capers of a white scarf which lifts the boat to the window isolates on the steps of the amphitheatre the plough and the furrow, which sacrifice solemnly the goat chained down to the immaculate paper of a great page of writing.

SECOND LITTLE GIRL: Let the goat graze, give her some cabbage leaves. You are stupid, you are stupid, really really you are stupid, stupid, stupid, stupid!

FIRST LITTLE GIRL: A mattress of brambles for me to sleep tonight on a syrup of blackberries. Skylark, gentle skylark, have you had a good breakfast?

(FIRST, SECOND AND FOURTH LITTLE GIRLS *silently start to run in every direction and catch each other, and doing so run up the steps leading to the first floor of the house.*)

THIRD LITTLE GIRL (*comes out of the well and jumps to the ground; she runs after the others, climbs the steps and goes in shouting*): Coming, coming, coming, coming, coming, coming, coming, coming...

ACT TWO

Scene: The same garden, but with a large boat in the middle. Tied to the boat is a goat. The stage is empty.

THIRD LITTLE GIRL (*comes down the steps from the house, holding a doll bigger than herself chained with garlands of flowers and leaves; a yellow apron*): White bird with amaranth-blue and lemon-blue checks, perpendicular line of sky-blue, irritating average of white spread on the lilac stain in great spoonfuls of broad lemon-yellow, spread body and soul on the closed ogive of the sparkling centre of a great circle, closed and double-locked with lacquers, emerald silence hidden between the folds of an egg laid by the goat.

(*She arranges her doll, chained with garlands of flowers, in the boat and ties it to the mast; lies on her back on the ground and sucks and caresses the goat.*)

Handsome young man, good-looking sweetheart, my lover, my sun, my passion, my centurion, my furious horse, my falsehood, my hands like spirals of butter, delicious ascent and descent attached to the chains of the merry-go-round at the fair, lemon squashed in the mouth closed with nitric acid of a tender dove that opens like a fan at the centre of the smoky furnace of a tar barrel.

(*She gets up, unties the goat and cuts its throat, takes it in her arms and dances.* FIRST, SECOND AND FOURTH LITTLE GIRLS *are at the window of the house, watching: for a moment they go inside, then come back with big moustaches painted on their lips and let go a number of pigeons that fly away. And the* FIRST, SECOND AND FOURTH LITTLE GIRLS *jump through the window into the garden; they have attached great open wings to their shoulders; they surround the* THIRD LITTLE GIRL, *holding the dead goat in her arms, and push her into the middle of their circle.*)

SECOND LITTLE GIRL: Show us the blind light of her ice-cold song and the aurora borealis of her fleeting glance, so that she will explode over us like bouquets of vipers, her haloes of jasmine and her hands full of signs!

FOURTH LITTLE GIRL: Let her blood run over my forehead, so that I can feel the coolness of the trade winds of her life that has flown away!

SECOND LITTLE GIRL: The marble slab of her glance decomposes like sequins of icy fire which boil in the indolent thrill of a crystallization of curves.

FOURTH LITTLE GIRL: Let's fetch some wine from the pitcher, from the great jars, let's bring all the wine, so that she will be drunk at her death, so that she will sing and laugh with us and love us!

FIRST LITTLE GIRL: The boat moves, swells, rises, it lights up all over, and a thousand arms row in fields of cobalt-blue, lemon, emerald-green, lilac, pink and poppy-purple, lees of white wine, sky-blue pink, iridescent pigeon feathers and lemon, tangerine, grapefruit and bitter green-orange juice.

SECOND LITTLE GIRL (*puts her little arm all the way into the wound of the slaughtered goat and pulls out the heart, which she shows to the other little girls*): It's alive – it's alive – it jumps – ha! It hurts, it bites me – pull it away from me – it jumps at my throat – it tears me – strangles me – kill it – kill it – it's alive.

FIRST LITTLE GIRL (*seizes the heart, with hands wrapped in a piece of her dress – and, as though she were holding a red-hot coal, she puts it into the mouth of the doll*): The heart will go and lay its egg and, at matins, the hive will chant its litanies of honey and of gall stuck to the rigging and the sails of the stranded ship, spume from the curls of the sun.

FOURTH LITTLE GIRL: Here the page is white, empty, snuffed out. Silence wraps its feet in ashes, a great soft white pool deposits its spit with pale fingers on the edge of the sheet stretched over the corpse.

SECOND LITTLE GIRL: The goat sleeps off its wine, dead in the swaddling clothes of milk spilt in a pool of blood, sunk into the mud up to the ankles of the open flower.

FIRST LITTLE GIRL: I am going to tidy up a bit, I am going to sweep away all this dust from the stars that we crush with our heels and water a little with our tears the great desire to laugh at that big mouth full of earth from the garden. You two, each with your knife, mend the large azure flagons all swollen with wisdom using all the gentleness necessary and desired, and let there be no trace of those bolts from crossbows scattered on the top of the tower crowded with howling cupids, flapping their wings through the bars.

SECOND LITTLE GIRL: There, there, look at the serpent, its sword goes so gently into the wound and does not tremble in its hand.

FIRST LITTLE GIRL: Laughter is dead, laughter will live, laughter has put on its wedding dress and adorned its hair with anemones, but the long veil made of lead immobilizes it and crushes it, and its train gets caught and splits and breaks the crystal cups full of flowers so delicately placed on the ground in its path.

SECOND LITTLE GIRL: Look, I filled this cup with water, I took away the glass, and the water stays in place without one drop wetting my hands. Now I have broken the glass, and I don't know where to put this water.

FOURTH LITTLE GIRL (*puts her lips to the water and drinks as though at a fountain*): How sweet and cool it is!

SECOND LITTLE GIRL: And clear!

FIRST LITTLE GIRL: Is it the tree of wisdom and good and evil or just a bit of nonsense?

SECOND LITTLE GIRL: Only the eye of the bull that dies in the arena sees.

FIRST LITTLE GIRL: It sees itself.

FOURTH LITTLE GIRL: The deforming mirror sees.

SECOND LITTLE GIRL: Death, that clear water...

FIRST LITTLE GIRL: And very heavy.

FOURTH LITTLE GIRL: Hem in the bed of slates with green leaves and cover the lace of crabs with myrtle making a private room and white secret alcove so gently I want to read to you deep in the woods from my account book and my accordion-pleated prayer book – the first notes written and sung radiantly and combed backwards drip their roses and periwinkles on the spider's web doing their accounts on the edge of the sink. I add, number one, a little bag of burnt almonds, mauve, pink and green, a carnival mask, a mask of ashes sweating years of pitch and stitched with a shower of grains of rice, lighting up the laughing side of a summer sky, bent just now round the grassy pole sucked in by the storm and, number two, adding with all its weight to the torn canvas which fans the embroidered muslin of the funeral pyre, the guts ripped out, soaking its fingers in the sea, the side of the vase full of jasmine and after that regiments of boring things – the butcher 50, the grocer 3,000 – coal, oil, peas and carrots, sugar, cloves, potatoes, onions, olives, salt, pepper 38 and 11 and 200, 3,000, 80, 650, rice, garlic, chickpeas, the orange flight of black doves behind the fan opened and thrown on the floor, long letter to answer and not to be read with eyes closed to tunes crossing their swords point to point and the long procession of herds of eagles, gnawing claw and beak into the back of a sheet covering the festive table and the torches.

FIRST LITTLE GIRL: The steel of fireworks crouched in a circle and the deployed acrobatic fables herborizing the azure azureal blue so tender and coaxing, dressed in blue of all the parsimony of its exposed anguish.

SECOND LITTLE GIRL: Happy birthday, happy New Year, lovely summer, metallic air, bees' tongues, smells of toast and butter and watermelon.

FOURTH LITTLE GIRL: At night, I sing and weep, my head knocking on the hinges of my bed. The arabesques of the skeins of wool of my palette stuffed with birds and my hands torn to ribbons tear to pieces bunches of anemones.

SECOND LITTLE GIRL: The merry song of being beautiful and very fat and a charming girl, unique piece and very rare, the thick white chalk lime will timidly cross out the bill.

FIRST LITTLE GIRL: The indigo chisel notched with emerald cuts the arch of the bridge in two from the square of the playing card shouting out its good luck, the shadow breaks its moorings.

SECOND LITTLE GIRL: Trees, jewel full of words, necklace of hopes, chain of honey, air of a flute, mask of clay, bell of pink silver, of crystal, sleep of a clock.

FIRST LITTLE GIRL: See how the sun who desires us comes to us through the leaves and makes lepers of our faces, our hands, our dresses and the garden. Its fingers smell of dried figs, pus, blood and spikenard, and the blue of its dress decomposes into a thousand sequins and Gregorian chants and alkaline mustiness.

(*Laughing*)

The sun is disguising us as corpses, the sun loves us.

* * *

SCENE OF THE GRAVEDIGGERS' CARNIVAL

A troupe of gravediggers arrives carrying a coffin. They are disguised as satyrs, centaurs and bacchantes. They come in dancing drunkenly, put the coffin on stools, which they cover with palm branches, open it and take out some big jars and cups, which they fill with wine and, while drinking, dance in a circle around the jars set up on the coffin.

SECOND LITTLE GIRL: Dance by night round the lights, sing the rainbow of a game of cards and keeping time tear from the strings of the jar its fire and silence in the palm of the hand.

FIRST LITTLE GIRL: Icicles of stars placed on the live fire of layers of sun suffering from its seaweed, architecture all in footpaths, egg laid cheaply, blue sheet burning at its four edges.

SECOND LITTLE GIRL: Ashes thrown as food to the eagles of the hen-run melt the bronze wings of the horse that draws the plough to a diamond song and chains the melodies of the point of the burin, scratching honey from the copper, to the lanterns.

FOURTH LITTLE GIRL: Organs drunk with mad love, anchors thrown to the bottom of the heavens, moorings hauled in from boats soaked in flames.

SECOND LITTLE GIRL: The big cherry tart is full of flies. If you don't want a taste, I eat it all myself, all, and afterwards you can weep, weep, weep and beat me.

FIRST LITTLE GIRL: The tart belongs to me as much as any of us!

FOURTH LITTLE GIRL: The tart belongs to nobody, or rather it belongs to the flies.

(*The* GRAVEDIGGERS *take up the coffin again with the same ceremony as on arrival and go out dancing: the* LITTLE GIRLS *follow them and the* THIRD LITTLE GIRL *is heard shouting:*)

Coming, coming, coming.

ACT THREE

Scene: The same garden, but the four little girls are naked inside a cage.

SECOND LITTLE GIRL: At hopscotch the trees are the bells of a plumb line which at each meal a tune on the violin carries off at each stop, and spins a web of violins sewn to the lilac fringe of a widespread group of hunters, of cobalt rocks and necklaces of sea urchins attached to each leaf overflowing on the stretch of wall near the clock, and the incompatible wounds and the whiplash of the aromatic leap of carp, of so much azure mixed with the guipure lace, of carnage and shame and rustling sorrow, of flowers fainting on the almond lake. To each lamb the weight of its wings and the heavy load of dawns brought to light on the marble engraved by claws and teeth, the melancholy innocence of rags, wiping sweat from the forehead of the blue sky, bound to the stake by the strings of the rainbow stretched to breaking point, finds its way to the bewilderment of the perfume and the lucky part of the feast.

FIRST LITTLE GIRL: The catastrophic absence of all scaffolding and the vague fear of the high jump from the top of the ladder plant a flag at the summit, unfurl their ceremonies and their birthdays.

(In the middle of the stage the bowl of a great aquarium appears, where coloured fish swim round; one is red, another blue, another yellow, another green, another violet, another orange. The bouquet of a firework display comes out of the aquarium.)

FIRST LITTLE GIRL (*continuing*): The ink from the fountain cuts its knees on the melted butter of this afternoon played heads or tails in the crystal prism of the persistently sour smell of the scrolls, the chants, the shadows gathered by hands stretched out for punishment and delicately convulses drop by drop the unbridled race of pink chariots of the ibises, dragging their rags in mud from the lime stirred by oars striking in disorder their palms on the watered silk of the arcades nailed body and soul to Ariadne's fan and thread, entangled, all feasting set aside, in the brambles of Roman eels.

FOURTH LITTLE GIRL: The shadow of dawn marks with its nail its bouquet of anemones on the corner of the page.

SECOND LITTLE GIRL: Rat, mouse, field mouse, shrew, bat, feverfew flower, grey balm, nitric acid set astride the lilac branch asleep, graciously settled on the cloven hoof of the contract in a rain of roses and cream tarts.

FIRST LITTLE GIRL: Round, spiral point thrown to the wind, lying in wait on the target, detached from the tree planted with its roots in the air on the emerald lake.

SECOND LITTLE GIRL: Scribbles, scribbles, scribbles wiping the sponge soaked in chalk over the air and the song, pinning the scarf of the moon to the landscape, shouting their heads off in delicate attentions and melancholy and agonizing contortions, rat, mouse, field mouse, shrew, bat, acid balm grey nitric lilac and distant rain of wings' beats hitting hard through the cage like fire on the bars of the sky.

FIRST LITTLE GIRL: Serpent plaited into long pigtails, each bee dressed in its robe of flowers, a mug full of milk leaps on each twig holding out a handful of forgeries and cascades of melody, arabesques and piercing bites.

SECOND LITTLE GIRL: The little ladybird crawls, its lanterns hung on a cord round the neck of the gallows, and squeaks its olive oil at the flints greasing the periwinkle blue pool, wiping the windows of its linen soaked in an egg breathlessly beaten into an omelette.

FIRST LITTLE GIRL: The little creature is dead, *ora pro nobis*, the little creature pops off, it has popped off.

FOURTH LITTLE GIRL: Some bread, a glass of wine and soup, the table spread with the dark-blue and light-blue check cloth, fork, knife, spoon, napkin folded on the plate, the punch from a fist in the right side of the table from the bucket of spilt yellow turned slightly pink, vomited by the sun wiping away the pearly colour spread facing it on its spurs.

SECOND LITTLE GIRL: Count – say 1, 2, 3, 4, 10, 11, 20, 2, 3, 4, 4, 4.

FIRST LITTLE GIRL: Count, count, count.

FOURTH LITTLE GIRL: Orange, tangerine, lemon, olives, little grilled fish, the ticking of the clock, the evening hour, the day, the morning, the dawn.

ACT FOUR

Scene: The same garden, by moonlight.

FOURTH LITTLE GIRL (*seated on a chair alone*): The morning soaks its allusions and its blond wagons with bitter acid drops, rampant stars with the black paws of axle trees, full stops and commas fixed at the unhooked casement window howling because of so much ochre and pale festoons unravelled in the cracks of dust, and streaks oiling the step to the well thrown on the fire, taming the sparkling grey, providing a gourd taken from the trap, its splashes of illusion and its deceitful allusion on the hidden wings of the curtains agitating its melodies and its cries to a hundred cardinal points and its sausages burning white hot intervening in the game, discovering the nakedness spread on the rafters of the almond tree in flower, tucking up the bed with all its finery and balms, let loose in a flight of doves into the yawning jaws of the sun crushed on the embroidered cloth like almonds in a plate of rice, silence made clear, lying in wait swollen with hilarious music its hortensias in floods of remorse and attenuating circumstances. Grinning snout, bending nails in its closed fist, distributing its pointed arches, keeping its accounts day by day, folding its splashes into a ball and its slates under the wing. A pile of aromas intoning its hymns and its stings, all sails set, at each door and all incantations allowed, the open cage unfolds its fan and gnaws the marble of its chain, the inscribed number hunts for its fleas in the sink, the little blue saucepan sleeps

37

leaning against the pink shadow made gratuitously at one leap kneeling, lying on the ground, the sham violet cuts the throat of the window dragged on the tiles of the kitchen floor by its hair, the table wetting its feet in the blood, showing open-mouthed the circle of its blue teeth, useless vows hang their wings on the nails bent with rust, the gravity of the hour corrupts its flesh in the clarity put in evidence and the flow of the clock authorizes its authoritative disgust at each step.

(*Enter an enormous winged white horse dragging its guts, surrounded by eagles; an owl is perched on its head; it stays for a short time in front of the little girl and disappears on the other side of the stage.*)

Luminous fountain of rainbow hair standing on end, hung from each finger of the necklace of steel feathers that wound the beast to death, the cluster of bows and curtsies and the alarm given, inflict their caresses on the screeching spread of azure diluted in all the milk spilt on the trembling mimosa branch, hiding the piece with whitish incantations and strange explosions, twisting out of shape the tiny achievements of the concentric fluttering images, the blue dress with the lilac blouse, such tender green in its skirt, rosy hands, yellow beating time, red ochre woken up with a start from a gradual drowsy dream, spread drop by drop, immobilized in the chalk, suspended in floods, dosing the mixture of agreed signs, they trace an open road for the aroma detached as a sentinel along its verge.

(*A little cat holding a canary in its teeth jumps from branch to branch and snow begins to fall.*)

Sheet from the bed folded diagonally festooned with carnations and irises, Uncle Tom's cabin covered with moons and slices of watermelon, seaweed birds, Tristan and Isolde in plaster, chain of roses and palm tree full of figs and rats, big shell, gold watch and book full of words crossed out, gnawed to bits by swarms of bees, the tree of good and evil set on fire at auction.

(*Enter* FIRST AND SECOND LITTLE GIRLS, *naked, holding big lighted cigars in one hand, dragging by the other an empty handcart; the* FOURTH LITTLE GIRL *bursts into tears and dances madly until she falls to the ground laughing, tearing her dress to rags.*)

FOURTH LITTLE GIRL: Boiling fat fallen from the stars inundating with its cherry stones the pink sheets of the fields of violets, grilling its feathers in the mirrors of the sun, sleeping its siesta with wings spread on the feather curtain hung by day, biting wholeheartedly at the bait. Fine plate of hot tripe, wine overflowing from the jars, coarse white bread, bunch of bees full of roses, swarm of hands nibbling the silk scarf embroidered with caresses and needlepoint, a drop of blood twisting its flame, dress with big lemon spots, almond-green, black and amaranth, joy thrown to the ducks and plumb line twisted into the brambles of the palm borders, folded carefully with blows from an axe struck so hard by the lips of the streamers, hung from the pikes shining through the gauze as well as all the blue spilt in floods so snappily, showing beak and teeth to the pink wound and golden festoon, the glory of all diminutive green chequered scents, the answer turning its back to the sun held tight in its claws, the immensity of sorrow spilt, hiding the window with its hands of mud.

FIRST LITTLE GIRL: Teeth clenched around the fist of the eagle's neck, the whip of its down catches each petal, with the most unexpected caresses and violent reflections, untuned to the arches of the bridge, bursting into tears its cavalcades, processions and unforeseeable suggestions of the innumerable attributes so obscurely put in evidence. Here is the bill: three packets of white cotton for sewing and darning dead centre the catastrophic image revealed by the acid, the knee lighting up the road of the scars at each step...

SECOND LITTLE GIRL: Lovely fried gudgeon, a dish of gnocchi, sweet pissaladière, clear voice of linen gnashing its teeth, hung out as an offering to the sun lying in the shadow under the plane tree.

FIRST LITTLE GIRL: The slice of melon grills its polar hunger by moonlight.

SECOND LITTLE GIRL: Milk of sweet almonds, grapes, figs, lettuce, melted gold, black olives, handfuls of laughs in bunches and grape juice of newborn stars, silver trumpets paddling in the lake. Clay vase overflowing with miracles hit by swarms of bees, unapproachable ladder detached from a house on fire sprinkling the meadow with large handfuls of salt.

FOURTH LITTLE GIRL: I would like to have a gold violet silk dress embroidered with silver, sewn with pearls, jasmine and gossamer, bordered with branches of mimosa, heliotrope, narcissi, carnations, ears of corn and my head surrounded in flames seen between the brambles, deliver love to carnage, open wings to madness, and garlands of big poppies to the sargasso seas. Thickset cloves planted on the pink seaweed leak floods of froth from sky-blue roses onto words burnt into the gold of the marbles covering the wings of the grill that envelop a nest of grass snakes.

SECOND LITTLE GIRL: Black feast, fine linen hung up to dry soaked in tears on the unmade bed crossed out at each sigh from the shutters.

FOURTH LITTLE GIRL: Lie made clear as it boils over on the hand snatched from a fate surrounded by signs, liquid architecture of the palace of marvels floated on a crystallized cloud that scrapes the field of violets licking the flame.

SECOND LITTLE GIRL: Violent storm imagined by the bouquet placed out of harm from a rain of apple stew, behind the vegetable rack under the sink, covering the gold border of the broken folds of its violet cloak, hands stretched out to the sweetness of agreed signs.

FOURTH LITTLE GIRL: Pauper's grave open to feasting, to games of skill, to graffiti that suddenly bring lakes into leaf startled to sleep by Ophelias.

FIRST LITTLE GIRL: Giving black birth on the tide of orchids scoring their games of chance on fixed tiles, on torn linen, nudging each other at the bricks they have dropped, the number winning a halo of streamers, the head beating its forehead on the paving stones of the temple reflected suddenly on the blind eye of the lake covered over with black, scratching the figure minutely with its nail.

FOURTH LITTLE GIRL: Silence put in irons, straitjacket, twisted nail, scrap of burnt fat stuck to the emeralds of the open throat of the wood pigeon.

(*The* THIRD LITTLE GIRL *is heard shouting*:) Coming, coming, coming…

FOURTH LITTLE GIRL: The ointment of the folded wings of the horse drawing the plough gnaws open the wound and scrapes the bite made in the dress by the drops of sunlight, singing of their heavy toads in the shade it offers.

THIRD LITTLE GIRL (*far away*): Coming...

FOURTH LITTLE GIRL: Glittering pike nailed in the middle of the sky hung with apple-green velvet, the pink in the flounces of the border tearing its fringes on the blackberry thorns.

SECOND LITTLE GIRL: Great white square bunched up like cotton of the silks of the mauve wings of some tufts of azureal herbs, idyllic thorns of whipped cream, blue of shot lace, wax colour of an arm leaning on the edge of the window cut out of the sky, unfolded like fields of oats on the black mantilla of plumb lines crossing their batons of wood painted in chrome-green, squeaking their avid and fastidious desires in the sleeping jars, smothered by the gum arabic of the alkaline songs of chained concrete, caught in the trap of moons, dragged in assault by smallholdings, torn from the tardy songs of nightingales.

FOURTH LITTLE GIRL: The burden of the wings carrying the handle of a pitcher suspended from the timetable of a little finger.

SECOND LITTLE GIRL: Fancy dress ball on a slate nibbled in silence.

FOURTH LITTLE GIRL: Furious horse tearing off strips of skin from the stretched cheeks of the lake, sounding through arum lilies the veiled trumpets of the unleavened bread of the Last Judgement.

SECOND LITTLE GIRL: Great basket full of plums, plaited with birds, the distant flute making itself at home on a slice of melon, lighting up the railings of a bunch of jasmine, whipping the sweet and tender image with blows like iron, hard enough to shrink the longest arm.

FOURTH LITTLE GIRL: Today the seventeenth day of the month of May in the year nineteen forty-eight, our father has taken his first bath, and yesterday, a fine Sunday, he went to Nîmes to see a bullfight with some friends, ate a dish of rice *à l'espagnole* and drank an oenological wine in a test tube.

SECOND LITTLE GIRL: Love spreads its lava on the rekindled fire of the sundials, the ark floats on wheels of flame, oil flows on the storm in floods, the boat beats its wings on the drum blackened with weeping, a spout of ash gathers its seaweed round the spikes wrenched from the reddened blue of the trumpets, infesting the lace thrown on the bushes discovered by the answers and threads, through each gift the blushing hopes of twigs broken into long leaves on the crooked masts, grunting smiles taken from the design painted on a dress, and its folded hands stuck to the broken branches of the boat, stray shots biting the fixed white page, sweet almond-green of the lemon tree washing the edge of a rag sticking out from the whitewood table, painted with ochre on each step whipped by the grain of rice of the morning sun, lifting a leg against a calcinated wall full of revelations.

FOURTH LITTLE GIRL: Oracle hung on misfortunes, oozing out its troupes of chameleons from the rafters of the storm, wringing out its wings on a soil bristling with pikes, advancing on the prey.

SECOND LITTLE GIRL: Blue pink and mauve and lemon of a bowl of milk shaken at the window in the morning.

FOURTH LITTLE GIRL: Mouth opening its eyelashes on the rope ladder, jogging on the stone sink some musical capers of airs learnt from the metallic lyres of herds of aromatic arabesques, stuck tooth and nail on the white-powdered cloth that licks the jar, heavy

43

constellation of responses with all curtains lifted to the choruses, dissolved in the cream poured on the nettles, drawn in big handfuls of salt from the tangled wig of the fat beanstalk pointed like big black olives on the slates.

SECOND LITTLE GIRL: Mirror...

FOURTH LITTLE GIRL: Silence stripped of the crowds of fiery silver lamps fanned into daylight, the dance that falls on the flower that drowns makes notes of its laughs in the palm of its hand while loosening the buckle of its sandal.

SECOND LITTLE GIRL: Laughter makes its nest, the grass sings, the earth cries out, winks and crawls its barcaroles at ingenious votive festivities, oiling the upsurge of its palms...

(*The curtain comes down for a few instants.*)

(*Change of scene: The stage is painted white; backcloth, wings, flies are covered with all the letters of the alphabet and large numbers painted in all colours. The floor is also painted in the same way. In the middle, a bed where the three little girls –* FIRST, SECOND AND FOURTH *– are lying. Some enormous winged dogs wander round the stage by the bed.*)

FIRST, SECOND AND FOURTH LITTLE GIRLS (*in the bed, singing*):
Ah ah ah ah ah! Love.
Ah ah ah ah ah! Death.
Ah ah ah ah ah! Life.
Ah ah ah ah ah! Laugh, let's laugh, laugh, will you laugh, death, love, life, love will you laugh; life will you laugh, death will you laugh, laugh so that I laugh, so that life death, love and you and death, life and love

laugh – laugh with us, we laugh with you, love to death,
death to life, life to love, life to death, life, death, love
all through life!

(*The little girls jump out of bed, naked. They lay out on
the ground a large blue lake surrounded with flowers and
bathe in it. From the middle of the lake the* THIRD LITTLE
GIRL *emerges, also naked; her hair is covered with flowers,
and her neck, wrists, ankles and waist are encircled with
flowers; she dances in the middle, holding the doll in her
arms and the goat on a lead. The winged dogs fly away. A
crowd of photographer-reporters enter and photograph the
scene from every side.*)

THE CURTAIN FALLS

ACT FIVE

Scene: The same garden. The FOUR LITTLE GIRLS *in little bright-coloured dresses. The ball of fire of a great bursting sun rolls on the stage, on the big lake that the little girls spread on the ground at the end of Act Four. Enormous ibises paddle in the water and fish our fish and frogs. The* LITTLE GIRLS *sing, dancing in a ring:*

> We won't go to the woods
> The laurels all are out…

FIRST LITTLE GIRL (*shouting*): Jeannette, come here!
SECOND LITTLE GIRL (*shouting*): Jeannette!
THIRD LITTLE GIRL (*shouting*): Jeannette!
FOURTH LITTLE GIRL (*shouting*): Jeannette!
SECOND LITTLE GIRL (*shouting*): Jeannette!
THIRD LITTLE GIRL (*shouting*): Jeannette!
FOURTH LITTLE GIRL (*shouting*): Jeannette, here, look
– the letter!

(*The* LITTLE GIRLS *begin to read a letter aloud:*)
My cabbages, my turnips, my carrots, my swedes, my green peas, my larks, I write to you from here a thousand leagues from any perceivable sign and from all ambiguity, light sweeping the flood tide of sails, hitting hard at the shutters. The daughter of the ironmonger brought into the world last night at the inn the resplendent joy of being mother to a fat chubby-cheeked babe seen by the X-ray, huge revelation, incredible sight, joyous discovery that the open angles of the white wings of doves have been dragging from one good soup to another round the rainbows broken up on the marble. The father and

mother are well, and the angels only arrive much later. We expect also your uncle with his little bitch, and the heavy expenses come later, when the roses have made their bouquets, and the piggish trick will be played without drums or trumpets and all the fires lit on the oven grill, stripped naked by so many bouquets offered in sacrifice to the nymphs that you are. And if I make you laugh, that's too bad! Tonight will make it clearer, and tomorrow the toothache of her fat cat can sing matins and vespers on the back of all the old and courteous civilities and offerings to the Holy Virgin. If your uncle knew that I have written to you, you would be covered with stinking sores from the nape of the neck to the ankles, and I think that's just the hors d'oeuvre. Goodnight, and as I kiss you I am helping myself to some of my little lentils. Your humble servant and your very tender and devoted servant, not likely to forget secretly the whole of my old thoroughly mouldy packet of excrement from the plate alive and brimming over with my gratitude.

FIRST LITTLE GIRL: Stinking baggage, fat turd, exquisite sewage…

SECOND LITTLE GIRL: Room full of farts…

THIRD LITTLE GIRL: Old drain marmalade, bag of bedbugs…

FOURTH LITTLE GIRL: Sandwich gilded with shit…

THIRD LITTLE GIRL: The pearly axe of flowers from the bouquet of a sheaf of anemones diluted in the azure of the flames and the delicate attention offered to the grinning mask of a basket of storms strung up to the gallows, the lyre string of its wings beating in the cage.

FOURTH LITTLE GIRL: Emptiness puts out its claws and bites into the veil hung in front of the image.

FIRST LITTLE GIRL: Silence stretches its limbs on the soap bubble of the dream, buried in antics spilt from palms, beaten hard enough to draw blood.

SECOND LITTLE GIRL: Light boils its games, its prayers and its crowns of thorns at the centre of the scarf.

FIRST LITTLE GIRL: The landscape repaints on the slate with big teaspoonfuls, shakes its fleas at each point of the equinoxes with cold gilding, nestling as foliage on the marble of mermaids, a trace of blue burnt as a sheaf of oats, like a rain of incantations and piercing laughs and graceful games.

THIRD LITTLE GIRL: Black mouth of the sun full of cinders...

FIRST LITTLE GIRL: Terrifying smell of a plateful of stars cooked in a frying pan...

SECOND LITTLE GIRL: Fat ox-swallowing frogs, fable of Uncle Tom and the flea-tamer Holy Virgin, the architect having done his jobs pulling away the ladder with both hands...

FIRST LITTLE GIRL: Window open to the immaculate white of a page marked in the centre in bees' honey with the word "laugh"...

FOURTH LITTLE GIRL: Milk of jasmine...

SECOND LITTLE GIRL: Ointment of spikenard...

FIRST LITTLE GIRL: Liquor of carnations...

THIRD LITTLE GIRL: Wide chalk line obstructing the road...

FIRST LITTLE GIRL: The hollow soup opens itself up in garlands of navels, and the fête begins again, seaweed, festoons and sprays in the alcoves, sweet milk drawn in the evening from the heart of the lake standing high on its stilts beating with its wings the sheets of the bed, scratching the milk-warm leaves with big ink marks.

SECOND LITTLE GIRL: The shadow of the lemon tree hollows out its nest on the point of a knife stung to the heart in the acid hidden underfield of sea anemones waking up.

FIRST LITTLE GIRL: Cool shadow hung from time drunk at the spring...

SECOND LITTLE GIRL: Salted anchovies of the wide road of memories, chopped small on the marble covered with graffiti from so many dawns, abandoned at the end of a row of cups full of blind nightingales...

FOURTH LITTLE GIRL: Nimble fingers of night singing drop by drop their necklaces of dew...

FIRST LITTLE GIRL: And the harp of each leaf riveted to each star caught in the robe, swinging in the folds of the illuminated merry-go-round with lights snuffed out by day...

SECOND LITTLE GIRL: Emerald filled with black pepper, drop of boiling wax fallen into the astonished eye of the night...

FOURTH LITTLE GIRL: Great oriental pearl stolen by a tarantula...

FIRST LITTLE GIRL: Circumference open to laughter...

SECOND LITTLE GIRL: Wild joy of fans let go like a flight of doves on the blue of a cheek...

FIRST LITTLE GIRL: Opening the silence of a slice of watermelon, freezing the time peeled dying from the nails, beaks, claws of acid-drop blue, keeping the pen marks from the bamboo balcony fixed like a streamer to the music that leaps wildly on the bed like voices offstage.

SECOND LITTLE GIRL (*diving into the lake and singing*): Silence of rose, silence of melon, silence of marshmallow, silence of coal, rose of silence, melon of silence, rose of silence of coal of rose, of rose of rose, of rose of white poppy, and the house, the fly on the green sleeve of the mauve dress with yellow polka dots, swallowtail hat, toad shoes, grass-snake belt, lovely amaryllis, pears, figs, peaches, oranges, lemons, fresh mountain air and a whole lot of old gits and *ora pro nobis* and say goodbye by showing my arse.

(Some big hogs and sows and their piglets, all winged, fill the lake. The LITTLE GIRLS *dance and sing in chorus the song that the* SECOND LITTLE GIRL *first sang alone – two or three times. Immobility. A great silence.)*

ACT SIX

Scene: In the vegetable garden, under a big table, THE FOUR
LITTLE GIRLS. *On the table, an enormous bouquet of flowers and some fruit on a plate, a few glasses and a jar, some
bread and a knife. A large serpent winds itself round one
of the legs of the table and rears up to eat the fruit, bite at
the flowers and the bread, and drink from the jar.*

THE FOUR LITTLE GIRLS (*reading a book*): The life of
life to life of life if life the life to life for life so life
to life the life the death to death so death the death
to death of life to death so life so death the life the
death to life of scented life, ladder pointed at the
tide of luminous squares of azure, in baskets, wild
cats, corollary in acid-watered opal and garlands
with the fragrant rifts of stippled and luminous
feasts, musicians' glances seen again so recently
revealed in the rents – orgasms of wings methodically
dissolved in balls and processions, ointments and
cavalcades – the open door of oblivion hitting its
stinking ponds against the sky – a piece of its torn
dress wiping the window panes, gumming together
the pile of revelations contained in the broken cup,
dissolving the aroma into fragile houses of cards,
scratching the ice from the mirror with clenched
fists – sham justified by the enormous sum to be
paid, and of which here are the details, the dress
made of wishes festooned with gold and jasmine,
all of pearl, belt of amaryllis sewn with diamond
thread, white lettuce watered drop by drop with
stars, great bouquet of fire at the Pont Neuf about

eleven o'clock at night on Bastille Day, jaw shut
and bolted of a lizard caught by the charm of the
stuttering wings of a nocturnal butterfly convuls-
ing with its arms in the cream of night diluted
in boiling marble chanting the full length of its
litany at the passing bait, great pile of onions, of
aubergines, of pimento, of melons and of figs, of
thyme, of rosemary, of seabass, of rascasse, of eels,
of garlic, moon robe with big emerald feet, white
robe of clouds, robe of azure, robe made of great
tree trunks, walnut, oak, mahogany, ironwood, ebony,
the castanet player, rose and lemon wood, liquorice
wood and Panama wood suitable for washing.

SECOND LITTLE GIRL: The rose of the carnation laughs
the story with all its teeth. It listens and reflects already
on the final consequences of threads plaited so finely to
make a screen and a clean sweep of all smothered rage
at the dawns so long awaited.

FIRST LITTLE GIRL: Everything lights up, my dress of
midsummer fire scribbles its horoscopes on my hands
and gives a drink of swords to the hordes of goats giving
birth on the wet grass.

(*A veritable ballet of winged ants fighting for their queen
in fantastic tournaments fills the stage from top to bottom.*)

FOURTH LITTLE GIRL: Glowing coal, fleur-de-lis seaweed
of the tide of musical blood from heavy river hung from
electric wires made of shells...

SECOND LITTLE GIRL: My hand detached from the
cheek falling headlong like an acanthus flower along
the arm plunging with all its prize of sheaves of
thorns in alabaster into caricatural harmonies, breaking point of an apparent wound made impromptu
by the lilac-white buttering at the end of its stork a

singular apparition drunk to the dregs from the marble
heart hidden behind a mask painted flesh-colour...

(THE FOUR LITTLE GIRLS *take the snake and, using it like
a big scythe, make sweeping blows in the air at the flying
ants and bring them down. Behind the garden, some young
boys pass, playing the accordion and singing:*)

> Oh! Little white wine that we drink in the shade
> Where the girls are lovely down our way in Nogent
> And then once again an air of old romance
> Returns to set us all swinging
> Down our way, down our way, down our way,
> Down our way, down our way in Nogent.

(*Great bursts of laughter.*)

(*The night falls. Some stars, the moon. All the stars.
Some crickets. Some frogs. Some toads. Some cicadas.
Some nightingales. Some fireflies. An intense perfume
of jasmine fills the theatre, and a dog is heard bark-
ing in the distance. Later, the whole garden lights up,
each leaf is a candle flame, each flower is a lamp of its
own colour, each fruit is a torch, and the ribbons of
the branches of the trees are lights of separate flames.
Shooting stars fall like harpoons from the sky and plant
their swords which open like roses and cups of fire.* THE
FOUR LITTLE GIRLS *play at leapfrog and laugh – laugh
and sing:*)

> Purée of potatoes, purée of lentils, purée of runner
> beans, purée of broad beans and purée of onions, cheers
> for the cream, cream of chestnuts, vinaigrette sauce,
> bitter-sweet apple, cabbages in cream, chocolate éclair,

plum tart, ginger bananas, melon, figs and peaches, apricots, grapes.

(*They lie down on the ground and go to sleep. Some trees, flowers, fruits; everywhere blood is flowing: it makes pools and inundates the stage. Four big white leaves, forming a square, grow from the earth and shut in* THE FOUR LITTLE GIRLS. *While turning, there appears by transparency written successively on each leaf:* "FIRST LITTLE GIRL", "SECOND LITTLE GIRL", "THIRD LITTLE GIRL", "FOURTH LITTLE GIRL".)

(*Complete blackout.*)

(*The stage after lighting returns: the interior of a cube painted white all over fills it completely. In the middle, on the ground, a glass full of red wine.*)

FINAL CURTAIN

Golfe-Juan, 24th November 1947 –
Vallauris, Friday 13th August 1948

DESIRE CAUGHT
BY THE TAIL

Characters

BIG FOOT
THE ONION
THE TART
HER COUSIN
ROUND PIECE
THE TWO BOW-WOWS
SILENCE
FAT ANXIETY
THIN ANXIETY
THE CURTAINS

ACT ONE

Scene One

BIG FOOT: Onion, stop being funny; now we are well feasted and ready to tell the four primary truths to our cousin. Once and for all we must explain the causes of the consequences of our adulterous marriage; we must not hide its muddy soles and its wrinkles from the gentleman rider, however respectful he may be of propriety.

ROUND PIECE: Just a moment, just a moment.

BIG FOOT: No good, no good.

THE TART: Enough, that's enough, quiet down and let me talk.

BIG FOOT: Well.

ROUND PIECE: Well, well.

THE TWO BOW-WOWS: Gua, gua.

BIG FOOT: I wanted to say that if we want to come to an understanding at last concerning the price of furniture and the letting of the villa, we must, and absolutely with one accord, strip Silence immediately of his suit and put him naked in the soup which by the way is beginning to cool off at a frantic pace.

FAT ANXIETY: I ask for permission to speak.

THIN ANXIETY: Me too, me too.

SILENCE: Will you shut up?

THE ONION: The choice of this hotel for private meetings in a walled-in public place such as this has not yet been made, and we ought to examine this very unsettled question under the microscope, bit by bit and between the finest down of its hairs.

BIG FOOT: Don't hide so cunningly behind the behind of the story which so deeply interests and grieves us; the choice of witnesses has been made – holy mackerel! – and well made. And as for us, we'll be quite happy to cut our pattern from the shadow cast by the bills owing to the landlord.

SILENCE (*taking off his clothes*): God, it's hot!

THE COUSIN: I have already put some coal on, just recently, but it doesn't heat up. What a bloody bore.

THE ONION: That chimney must be swept tomorrow; it smokes.

ROUND PIECE: It would be better to build a fine new young one next year... and that done, no more mice, no more black beetles.

THE TART: Me, I like central heating better; it's cleaner.

THIN ANXIETY: Oh! How bored I am...

FAT ANXIETY: Shut up, we're guests here.

ROUND PIECE: To bye-byes, to bye-byes... Do you know what time it is? A quarter after two.

Scene Two

(*Change of lighting to storm.*)

THE CURTAINS (*shaking themselves*): What a storm! What a night! Truly and certainly a night for cuddling... a Chinese night, pestilential night in Chinese porcelain... a night of thunder in my incongruous belly (*laughing and farting*).

(*Music by Saint-Saëns: 'Danse Macabre'. Underfoot the rain begins to pour upon the floor, and will-o'-the-wisps run about the stage.*)

ACT TWO

Scene One

A corridor in Sordid's Hotel.

(The two feet of each guest are in front of the doors of their rooms, writhing in pain.)

THE TWO FEET OF ROOM NO. 3: My chilblains, my chilblains, my chilblains.

THE TWO FEET OF ROOM NO. 5: My chilblains, my chilblains.

THE TWO FEET OF ROOM NO. 1: My chilblains, my chilblains, my chilblains.

THE TWO FEET OF ROOM NO. 4: My chilblains, my chilblains, my chilblains.

THE TWO FEET OF ROOM NO. 2: My chilblains, my chilblains, my chilblains.

(The transparent doors light up, and the dancing shadows of five monkeys eating carrots appear. Complete blackout.)

Scene Two

Same scenery.

(Two hooded men bring a huge bathtub full of soap suds onto the stage, in front of the doors of the corridor. After a piece for violin from Tosca, *from the bottom of the bathtub rise the heads of* BIG FOOT, THE ONION, THE TART, HER COUSIN, ROUND PIECE, THE TWO BOW-WOWS, SILENCE, FAT ANXIETY, THIN ANXIETY, THE CURTAINS.)*

THE TART: Well washed, well rinsed, clean, we are like mirrors of ourselves and ready tomorrow and every day once more to start the same merry-go-round.

BIG FOOT: Tart, I see you!

THE ONION: I see you.

ROUND PIECE: I see you, I see you, hussy!

BIG FOOT (*speaking to* THE TART): You have a pretty leg and a well-turned navel, an elegant waist and perfect tits, maddening eyebrows, and a mouth which is a nest of flowers, your hips a sofa, and the spring seat of your belly a box at a bullfight in the arena of Nîmes, your buttocks a plate of cassoulet, and your arms a soup of sharks' fins, and your... and your nest of swallows still the fire of swallow's nest soup. But my honey, my duck, my pet, you drive me crazy, crazy, crazy, crazy.

THE ONION: Old strumpet! Little whore!

ROUND PIECE: Where do you think you are, old man, at home or in a brothel?

HER COUSIN: If you go on like this, I shall refuse to wash, and I shall leave immediately.

THE TART: Where is my soap? My soap? My soap?

BIG FOOT: The hussy!

THE ONION: Yes, the hussy!

THE TART: How good this soap smells – oh, how good it smells!

ROUND PIECE: Take your sweet-smelling soap and stuff it up.

BIG FOOT: Beautiful baby, may I rub you?

ROUND PIECE: What a wench!

(THE TWO BOW-WOWS, *yelping, lick everybody. They jump out of the bathtub, covered with soap suds, and the bathers, dressed like everybody of this period, come out of the tub.* THE TART *alone gets out stark naked, except for her stockings. They bring in baskets of food, bottles of wine, tablecloths, napkins, knives, forks. They prepare a great alfresco lunch. In come some undertakers with coffins, into which they dump everybody, nail them down and carry them off.)*

CURTAIN

ACT THREE

Scene One

Black back curtains, black side curtains and carpet.

BIG FOOT: When you think it over, nothing is as good as mutton stew. But I am more partial, on a wonderful day when it is snowing hard, to having it boiled or well done *à la bourguignon* by the meticulous and jealous care of my cook, the Hispano-Moresque Slav slave, my albuminous servant and mistress, melting into the fragrant architecture of the kitchen. Apart from the pitch and the glue of her attentions, nothing can equal her allure and her chopped flesh on the dead calm of her regal movements. Her sprightly jokes, her warmth and her chill stuffed with hatred are nothing more, in the middle of a meal, than the goad of desire larded with gentleness. The cold of her nails turned against herself and the searing fire of her lips, frozen on the straw of the open dungeon, removes nothing of its character from the scar of the wound. The chemise lifted from beauty, her gaudy charm, anchored to her blouse, and the tidal force of her favours, shake off the golden powder of her glances into the nooks and corners of the sink, stinking of laundry hung out to dry at the window of her looks, sharpened with the whetstone of her tangled hair. And if the Aeolian harp of her foul and common language and her laugh trouble the polished surface of this portrait, it is due to her immoderate proportions and her disturbing propositions that she receives this avalanche of admiration. The spear from the bouquet of flowers, which she gathers in the air as she passes, shouts in her hands the royal acclamation of the victim. The galloping pace of his love, the canvas born each morning in the fresh egg of his nakedness, crystallized into thought, jumps the barrier and falls panting on the bed. I have such marks on my body; they are alive; they shout and sing and prevent me from catching the eight forty-five. The roses of her fingers smell of turpentine. When I listen at the ear of silence and see her eyes close, spreading the perfume of her caresses, I light the candles of sin with the match of her charms. The electric cooker can take the blame.

(*Knocking at the door*)

ROUND PIECE: Somebody there?
BIG FOOT: Come in!

Scene Two

ROUND PIECE: It is very comfortable in your place, Big Foot, old man, and what a good smell of roast sucking pig! Goodnight, I'm off. But crossing the Bridge of Sighs I saw a light in your place, and I dropped in to give you your ticket for tonight's draw in the national lottery.
BIG FOOT: Thank you. Here is the money. This is the sort of luck I had this morning, at biscuit time with figs – half fig, half grape, so fresh. One more day and it's black glory...
ROUND PIECE: It's cold!
BIG FOOT: Would you like a glass of water? That will warm your guts. This business of house-letting

preoccupies and saddens me because if the landlord, the good fat old Jules, agrees about the price and the fees, the neighbour from across the way, that bitch, worries me. Her fat cat never stops prowling round my cage of mice, and I can see the moment coming when the tropical fish that I feed to them alive will be torn to shreds and devoured by that stupid brute. My frogs of the tube game are in good health, but the aloe wine that I made has gone bad, and I cannot see this winter ending without greater shortages awaiting us.

ROUND PIECE: The quickest way would be to put a small dead mouse on the end of a solid fish-hook and, dragging the line gently on the end of a stick, lie down and wait until the fat cat is caught. Kill it, skin it, cover it completely with feathers, teach it to sing and mend watches. After that, you could roast it and make yourself a vegetable broth.

BIG FOOT: He who laughs last laughs best. Once the cat is dead and the person I love has come to wish me a happy New Year, the house will shine like a lantern and the feasting will burst all the strings of the violins and the guitars.

ROUND PIECE: Madness! Madness! Madness! Men are mad. The sash of the veil that hangs from the eye-lashes of the shutters wipes pink clouds on the apple-coloured mirror of the sky, which awakens already at your window. I am off to the café at the corner to tear off with my claws the remains of the chocolate colour that still prowls in the blackness of its coffee. A very good morning to you – till tomorrow evening, see you soon!

(*He goes out.*)

Scene Three

BIG FOOT *lies down on the ground in the middle of the stage and begins to snore. Enter from both sides of the stage* THE ANXIETIES, THE COUSIN *and* THE TART.

THIN ANXIETY (*looking at* BIG FOOT): He is as beautiful as a star. He is a dream repainted in watercolour on a pearl. His hair has the intricate arabesques of the halls in the palace of the Alhambra, and his complexion has the silver sound of the bell that rings the evening tango in my ears so full of love. His whole body is full of the light of a thousand shining electric lamps. His trousers are swollen with all the perfumes of Arabia. His hands are transparent mirrors made of peaches and pistachios. The oysters of his eyes enclose hanging gardens gaping at the words of his glances, and the aioli colour which encircles him sheds such a gentle light on his breast that the song of birds that is heard sticks to it like an octopus to the mast of a fishing smack which, in the swell of my blood, navigates according to his image.

FAT ANXIETY: I would like to have a go at him without his knowing.

THE TART (*with tears in her eyes*): I love him.

THE COUSIN: I knew a gentleman in Châteauroux, an architect who wore spectacles and who wanted to keep me. A very nice and very rich gentleman. He would never allow me to pay for my dinner, and in the afternoon, between seven and eight, he would have an appetizer at the big café on the corner of the high street. It was he who taught me how to fillet a lemon sole properly.

Afterwards, he went away for good, to live in an old historic castle. Well, myself, I find that lying like that on the floor and sleeping, they look exactly alike.

THE TART (*throwing herself on top of him and weeping*): I love him, I love him.

(THE TART, THE COUSIN *and* THE TWO ANXIETIES *each take big scissors from their pockets and begin to cut locks of his hair, until they have stripped his head like a Dutch cheese known as "tête de mort". Through the slats in the shutters of the window whips of sunlight begin to beat the four women seated round* BIG FOOT.)

THE TART: Aye aye aye aye aye aye aye.
THE COUSIN: Aye aye aye aye…
THIN ANXIETY: Aye aye aye aye aye…
FAT ANXIETY: A a a a a a a a a…

(*And that goes on for a good quarter of an hour.*)

BIG FOOT (*dreaming*): The marrowbone carts along blocks of ice.
THE COUSIN: Oh, isn't he beautiful! Aye aye aye… who aye… oh, who aye aye is aye aye aye aye… bo bo.
FAT ANXIETY: A a a bo a a bo bo.
THE TART: Aye aye I love him. Aye aye love bo bo aye aye aye love him aye aye bo bo bo bo.

(*They are covered with blood and fall fainting to the ground.*)

(THE CURTAINS, *opening their folds in front of this disastrous scene, immobilize their vexation behind a spread of unfolded cloth.*)

CURTAIN

79

ACT FOUR

Scene One

Stamping of feet.

THE TART: I'm going to win! You see, I'm going to win!

THE COUSIN: Me too! Me too! Me too!

FAT ANXIETY: I'll be first! I'll be the first!

BIG FOOT: I shall hit the jackpot.

ROUND PIECE: I shall get it!

THE ONION: Every time, I shall be first, you see, I shall be the first!

SILENCE: You will see, you will see!

THE ANXIETY: My little finger has told me!

(The lottery wheel turns.)

THE COUSIN: 7. That's luck! I hit the jackpot!

ROUND PIECE: 24. Plus 00,1042. But I hit the jackpot too! That makes 249 thousand 0089.

FAT ANXIETY: 9. It's my number all right that wins the jackpot.

THE TART: 60, plus 200, and one thousand and 007. I win it, the jackpot for me too! I have always been lucky.

BIG FOOT: 4,449, good God! Here we go, a millionaire, at the top of the list.

SILENCE: 1,800. Goodbye, misery, milk, eggs and dairy-maid! Here I am master of the jackpot.

ROUND PIECE: 4,254. Jackpot winner I am, congratulate myself.

THE COUSIN: 0009. I am the jackpot winner! I'm the jackpot winner! I am the jackpot winner!

THE ONION: 3,924. I win the jackpot! That's correct.
FAT ANXIETY: 11. That's the jackpot that I win!
THIN ANXIETY: 17,215. I've got the jackpot everywhere!
THE CURTAINS (*shaking themselves like madmen*): 1 – 2
    – 3 – 4. We win the jackpots! We win the jackpots! We
    win the jackpots!

(*Total silence lasting for some minutes, during which in the
prompter's box, over a big fire in a big frying pan, potatoes
are seen, heard and smelt frying in boiling oil; the fumes
of the chips fill the room more and more, until complete
suffocation ensues.*)

CURTAIN

ACT FIVE

Scene One

BIG FOOT (*half stretched out on a camp bed, writing*): "Fear of the uneven temper of love and tempers of the leaping goat of madness. Covering laid over azure released from the seaweed that covers the dress starched with rich scraps of flesh brought to life by the presence of puddles of pus from the woman who has suddenly appeared reclining on my bed. Gargle of the molten metal from her hair shouting with pain all her joy of being possessed. Random game of crystals embedded in the melted butter of her dubious gestures. The letter that follows step by step the word inscribed on the lunar calendar hanging by its folds from the brambles breaks open the egg filled with hatred and the tongues of fire of her will set in the pallor of a lily at the exact moment when the exasperated lemon melts with delight. Double game of knuckle bones painted with the same red as the border of her cloak, the gum arabic which drips from the calm of her attitude breaks the harmony of the deafening noise of silence caught in a trap.

"The reflection of her grimaces painted on the mirror open to the winds perfumes the hardness of her blood on the cold flight of the doves that receive it. The blackness of ink that envelops the rays of the sun's saliva, hitting on the anvil the lines of the drawing bought at the price of gold, develops, in the needlepoint of the desire to take her in his arms, his acquired strength and his illicit powers to win her. I run the risk of having her dead in my arms, ripe and mad." Love letter, if you like. Quickly written and quickly torn up. Tomorrow or this evening or yesterday, I will have it posted by the devoted care of my friends. Cigarette 1, cigarette 2, cigarette 3, one, two, three, one plus two plus three equals six cigarettes; one smoked, another grilled and the third roasted on the spit before the fire. Hands hanging around the neck like a rope let down in haste from a tree that flies away whip relentlessly her classic figure of a half-baked Venus. Both feet together, the day lowers the weight of these years into the pit, full of shadow. The guts dragged by Pegasus after the fight draw her portrait, on the whiteness and hardness of the gleaming marble of her pain.

The noise of unfastened shutters hitting their drunken bells on the crumpled sheets of the stones tears from the night despairing cries of pleasure. The hammer blows of flowers and the sweet stink from her tresses season the stew of her bay leaves and cloves. Flying hands, hands detached from the laced sleeves of the bodice placed and folded with such care on the velvet of the chair, propped so roughly against the cheeks of the axe planted on the block, copy mournfully in a fine round hand the lesson which has been learnt. Stone hardened with anemones that devour the quicklime of the curtain that sleeps on the ladder leaning against the sulphur of the sky hung to the window frame. The most valid reasons, the imminence of peril, the dread and the desires which drive her do not prevent her at a time of morose joy like this settling down comfortably at home on the hope-green sofa.

THE TART (*enters, running*): Good morning! Good morning! I bring you an orgy. I am all naked, and I am dying of thirst. Will you please make me a cup of tea at once and some honey on toast? I am ravenous and so hot! Please allow me to make myself at home. Give me a fur full of moths so that I may cover myself.

And to start with, kiss me on the lips, and here, here, here and there and everywhere. Isn't it clear that I must love you, to have come like this in slippers, like a neighbour, and all naked to say good morning and make you believe that you love me and want to have me close to you, darling little sweetheart that I am to you and absolute mistress of my thoughts for you, such a tender adorer of my charms you would seem to be? Don't be so embarrassed, give me another big kiss. And a thousand more. Go on now, go and make me some tea. And meanwhile I am going to cut the corn on my little toe that annoys me.

(BIG FOOT *takes her in his arms and they fall to the ground.*)

THE TART (*getting up after the embrace*): You're smart enough at giving and taking. I'm covered with snow and shivering. Bring me a hot brick!

(*She squats in front of the prompter's box and, facing the audience, pisses and pisses scalding hot for a good ten minutes.*)

THE TART: Oof! That's better now!

(*She farts, she farts again, she tidies her hair, sits down on the floor and begins a clever demolition of her toes.*)

BIG FOOT (*enters again, holding a big account book under his arm*): Here is your tea. No water in the tap. No tea. No sugar. No cup nor saucer. No spoon. No glass. No bread and no jam. But here under my arm I have a fine surprise: **my novel,** and from this great sausage I am going to cut you some thick slices, that I shall stuff into your head, if you will allow me and are willing to listen to me very attentively, during a few of these long years of blackest night that we are spending together cheerfully, this morning until midday. Now here is page 380,000, which to me appears to be seriously of interest.

(*He reads:*)

"The acrid stench spread around the concrete fact of the narrative, established a priori, does not pledge the person destined to this task to the slightest modesty. In the presence of his wife and before a public notary, we, the only responsible person established known and honourably recognized as author, I pledge my entire responsibility only in the specific case when unbounded anxiety may become fanatical and murderous for the limited view of the subject at table, expatiating at full capacity, on the plumb line of the complex machine for establishing at any price the exact data of this case already experimented by others, contrary to the light cast by points of view on how to support the weight of these interior precisions."

"The armoured ballroom was full of the sugar and the brine of beauty and the best of the darlings of select society seated facing reality full of the purple feathers of children thrown to the winds like out-of-date and worm-eaten tears."

"On the regimental clock tower, the clock advertised the most complete indifference to the angles of the sundial held at its waist. The titillations of crows that make the jagged wheel of the machine for sewing and unsewing buttons animate the half-dead landscape so little that grass grows over their flight and at the shadows carried by their wings fail to stick on the wall of the church, but slip along the cobble stones of the square, where they break to pieces in a satisfactory realization of the adventure which is destined to occupy this provisional pigeonhole."

THE ONION and THE COUSIN (*entering*): Oy... We have brought you some shrimps! Oy... look here... we have brought you some shrimps!

BIG FOOT: That's delightful; here we are having a quiet fuck, and you come and annoy us with your filthy shrimps. How do you expect us, Onion, and you, Cousin, to care a damn for your shrimps?

THE COUSIN: What? Rosy shrimps! Flowers! You call that "our filthy shrimps"? We are kind, we think of you, and you swear at us. That isn't nice.

THE ONION: That'll teach me next time to offer you shrimps.

BIG FOOT: No, but sometimes...

THE COUSIN: You, Tart, this time I shall go straight and tell your mother everything. This is fine and dandy! All naked in front of a gentleman, an author, a poet... and all naked in your stockinged feet, it may be very highbrow and very saucy, but that will not make you a Venus, nor a muse, nor give you the manners expected of a respectable girl. What will your mother say when this evening at the laundry she is certain to hear about this shocking, shameless behaviour of a trollop dragged in the gutter of **Big Foot's artistic studio** by her lewd desires?

THE TART: Cousin, you're a curse... and, by the way, have you any cotton wool? Otherwise lend me your handkerchief. I shall go and tidy myself and then go out. I'm off. I'm going home. Really this man is a pig, a pervert, a libertine and a Jew.

(*She goes into the bathroom.*)

BIG FOOT: Now that the Tart is gone, listen to me. That girl is mad and is trying to impress us with her affected tricks like a princess. I love her, of course, and she pleases me. But between that and making her my wife, my muse or my Venus, there is still a long and difficult path to reconnoitre. If her beauty excites me and I am mad about her stench, her table manners, her way of dressing and her affectations are a pain in the arse. Now, tell me frankly what you are thinking. I am listening. You, Cousin, what do you think?

THE COUSIN: I know her very well, your little friend. We were bosom friends at school for several years. And I can assure you that her conduct during lessons was held up to us as an example. If she was covered with spots, of course I knew all about that, that was not her fault, but because of a lack of various fatty substances and her negligence as a girl abandoned entirely to her instincts. Very dirty in her person, untidy hair, stinking of a thousand nasty smells and sleepy. In her short black apron, her heavy slippers and her knitted jacket, all the men – old workmen, young men and gentry – we could see clearly the fires and the candles lighted before her devastating image that they carried away, the pure diamond of the fountain of youth burning in hands hidden in their trouser pockets.

THE ONION: That child for me had the flavour of angelica.

THE COUSIN: Now, there's no denying it! The Tart is a big girl and quite a pretty girl.

BIG FOOT: Her body is a summer night overflowing with light and the perfume of jasmine and stars.

THE ONION: You like her, Big Foot. Big Foot, that is your business. If you like her, that's fine, and yours the luck, good and rotten. Courage! I give you my blessing. And

good luck and plenty of it! Are you coming, Cousin?
We are off. Well! Big Foot, no grudge against me...
The shrimps, don't forget to put in, specially, a big
piece of bacon rind, parsley and a good glassful of
donkey's milk.

THE COUSIN: ...'Night, Big Foot!

(*They go out.*)

BIG FOOT: What a set of pitiful prats.

(*He lies on the bed and begins to write again.*)

"The soft blue of the bow which covers with its lace
veil the roses of the naked body of a wild amaranth
in a cornfield soaks up, drop by drop, the load of little
bells from lemon-yellow shoulders beating their wings.
Already the Demoiselles d'Avignon have an income of
thirty-three long years."

THE TART (*comes out of the bathroom dressed and wearing
a hat after the latest fashion*): What, they have gone?
Without saying a word. In the English style. May I tell
you all these people disgust me! As for me, I love only
you. But we must be good, my great big everything.
Now that I am really a virgin, I am off straight away to
put up the luminous signs of my breasts within reach
of everybody, and feather my love nest in the all-night
city market.

BIG FOOT (*stretched on his bed and feeling underneath for
the pot which cannot be found*): I carry in my worn-out
pocket the candy sugar umbrella with outspread angles
of the black light of the sun.

CURTAIN

ACT SIX

Scene One

The scene takes place in the main sewer bedroom kitchen and bathroom of the villa of THE ANXIETIES.

THIN ANXIETY: The burn made by my unhealthy passions stokes the wound of the chilblains enamoured of the prism which has come to stay on the mauve angles of the rainbow and evaporates it in confetti. I am nothing but a congealed soul, stuck to the window panes of the fire. I beat my portrait against by brow and cry the merchandise of my pain at windows closed to all mercy. My chemise, torn to shreds by fans starched with my tears, bites the seaweed of my arms with the nitric acid of its blows, dragging my dress at my feet and my cries from door to door. The little bag of sweets that I bought yesterday for Big Foot for 40 centimes burns my hands. Festering fistula in my heart, love plays marbles between the feathers of his wings. The old sewing machine which turns the horses and the lions of the tangled merry-go-round of my desires chops up my sausage flesh and offers it alive to the ice-cold hands of stillborn stars, tapping on the panes of my window their wolfish hunger and their oceanic thirst. The enormous pile of logs waits resigned to its fate. Let us make the soup.

(Reading from a cookery book)

A half quarter of Spanish melon, some palm oil, some lemon, some broad beans, salt, vinegar, breadcrumbs; simmer gently; skim off as it rises, any soul likely to go to hell; cool off; print off a thousand copies on Japanese imperial and let it congeal in time to give it to the octopuses.

(*Shouting down the sewer hole of their bed*)

Sister! Sister! Come here! Come and help me to lay the table and to fold this dirty linen stained with blood and excrement! Hurry up, sister, the soup is already cold and melts on the bottom of the looking glass on the wardrobe. All afternoon I have embroidered in this soup a thousand stories, which it is going to whisper in secret in your ear if you will kindly keep until the end of the bouquet's architecture some violets for the skeleton.

FAT ANXIETY (*all dishevelled and black with dirt, rising from the bedlinen full of potato chips, holding an old frying pain in her hand*): I come from far away and am dazzled by how patient I had to be behind the hearse, jumping like the carp that the fat dyer and cleaner, who is so exact in his accounts, tried to place at my feet.

THIN ANXIETY: The sun.

FAT ANXIETY: Love.

THIN ANXIETY: Aren't you beautiful!

FAT ANXIETY: When I left this morning from the sewer of our house, immediately, just outside the gate, I took off my heavy pair of hobnailed shoes from my wings, and, plunging into the icy pond of my sorrows, I let myself drift in the waves far from shore. Lying on my back, I stretched myself out on the filth of that water and for a long time I held my mouth wide open to catch my tears. My closed eyes also received the crown of that long rain of flowers.

THIN ANXIETY: Dinner is ready.

FAT ANXIETY: Here is to mirth, love and the spring!

THIN ANXIETY: Come along, carve the turkey and help yourself properly to the stuffing. The great bouquet of terrors and frights already begins to wave us goodbye. And the mussel shells chatter their teeth, dying of fear under the frozen ears of boredom.

(*She takes a piece of bread, which she dips into the sauce.*)

There is not enough salt and pepper in this slop. My aunt had a canary which sang old drinking songs all night.

FAT ANXIETY: I shall help myself to some more sturgeon. The bitter erotic flavour of these delicacies keeps my depraved taste for spiced and raw dishes panting eagerly.

THIN ANXIETY: I found just now the white lace dress that I wore at the White Ball, which was given me on that disastrous day, my birthday, all moth-eaten and covered with stains, on the top of the W.C. cupboard, writhing in burning pain under the dust of the tick-tock of the grandfather clock. Without doubt our charwoman must have worn it the other day to go and see her man.

FAT ANXIETY: Look, the door comes running towards us. There is someone inside it who is coming in. The postman? No, it is the Tart.

(*Speaking to* THE TART)

Come in. Come and eat with us. You must be happy. Tell us the latest about Big Foot. The Onion came here this morning, pale and in despair, soaked in urine and wounded, pierced through the forehead with a pickaxe. He was weeping. We cared for him and consoled him as best we could. But he was in pieces. He was bleeding everywhere and screaming incoherent words like a lunatic.

THIN ANXIETY: Do you know, the cat had her kittens last night.

FAT ANXIETY: We drowned them in a hard stone, to be exact in a beautiful amethyst. It was fine this morning. A bit cold, but hot all the same.

THE TART: You know, I have found love. He has all the skin worn off his knees and goes begging from door to door. He hasn't got a farthing, and is looking for a job as a suburban bus conductor. It is sad, but go to his help... he'll turn on you and sting you. Big Foot wanted to have me, and it is

99

he who is caught in the trap. Look! I have been out in the
sun too long, I am covered with blisters. Love. Love… Here
is half a crown, change it for me into dollars and keep for
yourselves the crumbs of small change. Goodbye! For ever.
Happy birthday, my friends! Good evening! A very good
day to you! Happy New Year and goodbye!

(*She lifts up her skirts, shows her behind and, laughing, jumps
with one bound through the window, breaking all the panes.*)

FAT ANXIETY: A pretty girl – intelligent, but peculiar. All
that will come to a bad end.
THIN ANXIETY: Call everybody.

(*She takes a trumpet and sounds the "fall-in". All the characters of the play come running.*)

You, Onion, come forward. You are entitled to six
drawing-room chairs. Here they are.
THE ONION: Thank you, madam!
FAT ANXIETY: Big Foot, to you, if you can answer my
questions, I shall give the hanging lamp from the dining
room. Tell me, how much does four and four make?
BIG FOOT: Too much and not a great deal.
THIN ANXIETY: Very good!
FAT ANXIETY: Very good!
THIN ANXIETY (*uncorking a bottle and holding it under
the nose of* ROUND PIECE): Round Piece, what does
this smell of?

(ROUND PIECE *laughs.*)

THIN ANXIETY: Very good! You've guessed. Here is this
box full of quill pens. They are for you. And good luck.
FAT ANXIETY: Tart, show us your accounts.

THE TART: I have 600 litres of milk in my sow-like breasts. Some ham. Some streaky bacon. Some liver sausage. Some tripe. Some blood sausage. And my hair covered with chipolatas. I have mauve gums, sugar in my urine and egg white all over my hands, gnarled with gout. Bony cavities. Bile. Cankers. Fistulas. Scrofula. And lips twisted with honey and marshmallows. Clothed with decency, clean, I wear with elegance the ridiculous dresses that are given me. I am a mother and perfect whore, and I can dance the rumba.

THIN ANXIETY: You shall have a can of petrol and a fishing rod. But first you must dance with us all. Start with Big Foot.

(*Music plays, and they all dance, changing partners all the time.*)

BIG FOOT: Let us wrap the worn-out sheets in the face-powder of angels and turn the mattresses inside out in the brambles. Light all the lanterns. Throw flights of doves with all our strength against the bullets and lock securely the houses demolished by bombs.

(*All the characters come to a stop on either side of the stage. By the window at the end of the room, bursting it open suddenly, enters a golden ball the size of a man, which lights up the whole room and blinds the characters, who take handkerchiefs from their pockets and blindfold themselves and, stretching up their right arms, point at each other, shouting all together and many times:*)

ALL: You! You! You!

(*On the golden ball appear the letters of the word "Nobody".*)

Paris, Tuesday 14th January 1941

MORE 101-PAGE CLASSICS

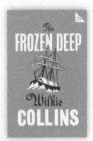

FOR THE FULL LIST OF
101-PAGE CLASSICS VISIT
101pages.co.uk

ALMA CLASSICS

ALMA CLASSICS aims to publish mainstream and lesser-known European classics in an innovative and striking way, while employing the highest editorial and production standards. By way of a unique approach the range offers much more, both visually and textually, than readers have come to expect from contemporary classics publishing.

LATEST TITLES PUBLISHED BY ALMA CLASSICS

www.almaclassics.com